I dedicate this book to a close friend who has helped me through both the good and bad times. Her vast spiritual knowledge has given me insights, explanations and often challenged my own preconceived views. More importantly, she gave me hope, laughter, immense comfort and reassurance when I really needed it. This person is a dedicated, talented, trance medium, who continues to perfect her development with the spirit world, in the simple hope to put more love and light back into this world.

Becky, thank you for being such a good friend!

THE RELUCTANT MEDIUM PART 3

Jane Lee

Copyright © 2024 Jane Lee

All rights reserved

Jane Lee has asserted her right to be identified as the author of this Work in accordance with the Copyright, Design and Patents act 1988.

No part of this book may be reproduced, or stored in a retrieval system, or transmitted in any form or by any means; electronic, mechanical, photocopying, recording, or otherwise, without express written permission of the publisher.

ISBN-13: 9798334453852

Cover design by: Gareth van Rensburg
Library of Congress Control Number: 2018675309
Printed in the United States of America

CONTENTS

Dedication	
Title Page	
Copyright	
Introduction	1
The Healing continues	3
I Decided to Take a Break	16
It Seems, There was a Purpose to the Sound Bath	29
Back in the Real World	37
Life is Good	39
A Day of Joy	42
Didn't See This One Coming	48
Time to Investigate	54
Try Explaining That One	68
An Alarmed Friend	75
Soul Removal	79
What is Going On?	90

Here We Go Again	95
Time to Push the Boundaries of What I've Been Taught	106
The Pace is Picking Up	118
I'm Becoming Braver	124
I'm Sat Stuck on the Fence	134
So, What Should I Do?	137
Confirmation	139
Going into the Unknown	142
Give Me a Break	148
Calmer Waters	154
A Refreshing Change	163
Here We Go Again	169
Drumming Circle	175
Hold it Together, Jane	185
I'm Taking a Break	191
Face to Face	194
What Have I Done?	200
Poor Lottie	203
What the Hell!	208
Time to Catch My Breath	214
Mind Over Matter	220
Hanging Out Dirty Laundry	225
Too Much Information?	231
An Interesting Conversation	234

A Lesson I Must Learn to Progress Forwards	242
An Angel is Sent My Way	246
The Healing Time Has Arrived	253
Life Continues	261
Holiday Time	263
Breathing Space	282
Give Me a Break!	284
Back Home	286
The Healing Session	288
The Veil is Thinning	292
Never Doubt Spirit	296
Fears Surfacing	304
The Tide is Turning	308
Adapting Takes Time	312
A Pleasant Surprise	314
Forgiveness Takes Time	321
A New Member	325
Contacted Out of the Blue	329
The Day of Reckoning	332
Returning to the Spirit World	345

INTRODUCTION

For many, you will already know I was born with the ability to see the spirit world. To be a medium was not exactly an inspiring dream of mine. I have overcome huge obstacles of self-created doubt and fear. Somewhere along the journey, I have finally started to accept and trust in a higher divine source. Through many mistakes and not fully trusting I, in fact learnt, anything can be achieved. These words are for us all.

My journey has been unconventional and sometimes frightening. However, it has also been uplifting, loving and incredibly healing. I have been guided to work in many spiritual disciplines ranging from psychic/mediumship, channel writing, and an array of healing methods, including Shamanism.

It wasn't until I stumbled across Shamanism that I discovered what true freedom felt like. The self-created cage of fear I had been fuelling was finally tamed. Through the process, I discovered the exact dimension/place, and spiritual healers I was meant to work with all along. The story continues.

In the final part of the story, both you and I

will know exactly my fate at the end. I know the journey ahead, but I am still unaware of the final piece of the jigsaw. We will both have to wait for the final twist, as I have all along been ensured it will occur.

Is all this fact or fiction? A higher divine intelligent source or merely a delusional woman? You the reader will have the final opinion as you have had all along. I simply tell my truth and if nothing else, open the minds of a few. Enjoy!

THE HEALING CONTINUES

It truly fascinates me how the spirit world picks out who needs healing and how they find you. I do not promote myself on social media as a healer, spiritual reader, or whatever it is you want to describe my work as. I'm frequently told by my spirit team that my time will come when I will have more opportunities to help others. But for now, I must stay focused on my writing. As much as I love spending time in the quiet, I also enjoy meeting new people. More importantly, I love working with spirit to help them.

I've learnt the hard way and know I must stay focused and disciplined to get these books completed before doing what fills my heart with joy - healing! I can't afford to complicate my journey or my health. So I continue with my written work and only heal when I'm contacted, usually through word of mouth. I've also noticed I don't get straightforward cases and usually it involves removing curses and entities. Yes, I just admitted to that and although hard to believe, unfortunately it is true.

Many people have usually gone around in circles for many years trying to find conventional medical methods before they stumble across me.

I suppose I'm a last resort, which is how it should be. Ill health should always be treated by medical professionals first and I'm a great advocate of that. Health is not only precious, but it is the most precious gift of all. A healer should only be contacted after exhausting all other avenues. Not as a substitute.

Anyway, I was contacted by a friend of a friend whether I would be willing to do distant healing for a terminally ill lady. Medically and scientifically, there was nothing I could do to help this person. I suddenly thought of my old friend and medium mentor, Eddie. I could hear the words of Eddie within my head saying, "Jane, you cannot heal everyone." Yet there was something inside of me that said I needed to.

I asked my spirit guides whether I had permission to help this lady as I knew it was going to be very challenging. Also, did I really want to get emotionally involved with a stranger who had limited time? I was told quite firmly this had been engineered, I was protected, and it was vitally important for this lady's future journey. "What the hell does that mean?" I thought.

So I did what I was told and contacted this lady who was in a lot of pain. What's even more upsetting was she was so young. I explained there was no scientific evidence in my healing technique, but if she was happy for me to work on her, then I would. Throughout the healing sessions, this lady continued with all her hospital and medical treatments. At the end of each healing session, my healing team would tell me if I needed to do another session.

The healing helped her a little. I suppose, I gave her hope but why were my spirit team insisting I continue healing her? Four weeks had passed. I had done some extreme healing within her body but yet no major improvements. I knew this lady was terminally ill, so why were the spirit world insisting on me working with her? You learn through experience just to trust. If they wanted me to continue, then I would.

On the fifth session of healing, I noticed the energy in the room had shifted from a pleasant gentle vibration to one of seriousness. It felt cold and sterile. Strange choice of words but true. As I started blending with my healing team and entering into her energy, I felt pure evil not only surrounding her, but within her entire body. I was shown her as a baby within the womb and a curse had been placed upon her mother.

I don't know whether it was in this lifetime or one previously. I'm a little startled as I've never witnessed anything like this before. I'm firmly told to concentrate and return to the healing, this is not the time to start overanalyzing. I'm taken to her belly button where I'm shown this string-like cord entering through this area towards her back, wrapping and twisting within her spine.

The cord, curse thing had wrapped itself throughout and deep within her spine. I feel my guides step closer towards me and immediately see my Indian guide place his hand over mine to let me know I am part of the process, not in charge of the outcome. I sense another healing guide coming in to help with the process. He is a surgeon, advanced in technology and procedures which man has not discovered yet.

Unassuming, slender, middle-aged, with a bald head and glasses. Again, I can't quite make out his facial features, but I know he is the best in his field of surgery. As he steps in, he guides me towards the spine, we need to find the top of the cord. The cord has entwined itself to the top of her neck and must be excruciating for this poor lady. It looks angry, menacing and evil. I don't know what it is, but it shouldn't be in her body. It's not part of her anatomy and physiology or dare I say, of this time.

We have found the top of this stringy substance and now need to start unravelling it. It feels like eternity as we gently weave in and out of her spine, gently removing the snake-like, stringy object. We must be precise so as not to affect or damage the surrounding tissues. More importantly, her spinal column. The intensity is off the spectrum, it feels like we have been working inside this lady's body for hours.

I feel tense, hardly daring to breathe as there is no space for error. Finally, we pull and weave this snake, cord-like, thick string to the bottom of the spine and then we manoeuvre it through the lower pelvis towards the belly button. Finally, I can see it coming out of this area, there are loads of it. Piles of this substance that seems to have grown larger over the years within this lady's body, literally draining her of energy and life.

As it's all removed, I'm shown a swirling funnel of air where it is sucked into and directed to the correct dimension where it will be dealt with and can no longer do harm to anyone. I breathe a sigh of relief, before we go back in to check over our work. Nothing can be left unprotected; the spinal cord is calmed down with a blue cooling substance administered by another guide who works as part of the healing team.

I call this healer Blue. Blue doesn't present as human, which I initially found hard to process, and a bit of a shock at first before deciding, it is what it is. For my own sanity, after seeing the healing benefits, accuracy and strength of Blue's work, I came to my own conclusion.

Blue is here to heal, nothing more, nothing less. I have no right to judge anything, especially a pure healing source.

Then another guide steps into my energy, working through me, to put a grey clay substance around her spine to ensure strength and stability. More importantly, it won't allow her energy to seep out, fatiguing her. Finally, gold light flows through the lady's body to ensure the process of healing continues until completed. The healing process ends. What the hell has just happened?

My analytical mind is starting to go into overdrive. No! First, I must disconnect fully, remove myself completely out of this lady's energy, and then straight away go back up to the higher world to be cleansed properly. I can't afford to have any of that, anywhere near me. I travel up and I'm immediately greeted by my healing team who are all over excited by what has just taken place.

It literally feels like a huge celebration, cheers of joy and love, it feels blissful. I'm filled with a sense of heightened euphoria and so much love, I feel tearful. The spirit world is congratulating me for my bravery and selfless act to help another. Not a friend or a loved one but a fellow human who I didn't personally know. And I had put myself in harm's way to do what I thought was right.

I knew immediately this had been engineered to

help this lady. But unfortunately she wouldn't get the full benefits in this lifetime, but in her next. Without the removal of that curse, or whatever you want to call it, she would be bound to it in the future. Get your head around that one, blimey! As I stood surrounded by my healers, who I know individually rather well. I suppose I should explain I have a team of six.

There is the main healer who presents himself to me as an Indian healer who was in a previous time, also my grandfather. He taught me things I wasn't aware of until I stumbled across Shamanism. I have a very powerful well-known healer in front of me, to my left. His presence is pure healing love. He watches from a distance and only enters my energy when it is vital to help others.

An African medicine healer behind me again on the left. He is handsome, black, vibrant, full of optimism, and has loads of energy. He wears some sort of animal fur over the top of his head, but I can never work out what the animal is. He is extremely powerful and is capable of removing dark energies. To my right is Blue, a blue swirling energy who looks like how you would imagine an alien.

I can't believe I've just admitted to that but it's the truth. Blue as I have named it, can take all inflammation and pain away. Next to blue is a normal looking bloke, who is bald, slender and I can see glasses but not fully his face. He is an amazing healer and can administer surgery that hasn't been invented.

Finally, to the right and at my back is a woman who seems very familiar. She has mousy brown, shoulder length hair. Once again I am not permitted to fully see her face. This lady is very familiar, perhaps I know her from another time? She is like a gatekeeper. I have discovered I can ask for specific healers to enter, for example a knee specialist. If it is safe, she will let them have access.

Well, I sound completely normal after admitting to that. NOT! Well, I said I would tell the truth. It's my truth so make of it what you wish. The funny thing is, I know there will be many who can relate to this, just haven't been silly enough to admit to it. I digress, so as I said I'm standing surrounded by my healers when they start to step back and gesture that I need to move forwards.

Directly in front of me is a dark blue door which is slightly open. I can't see anything, just a swirly, smoky substance. I understand this sounds ridiculous to some of you, but like you would imagine being in a cloud. I notice my guides remain where they are, as though they haven't been given permission to enter. I'm completely calm, unfazed and happy to enter. Again, this is all comforting, knowing and familiar.

As I push open the door, all I can see is pure white – a completely white room. I can feel there are many people in the room as it feels busy, but calm. I'm not given permission to see any of their faces, yet once again, I know I have been here several times before. I recognise one lady who I have been visited by before in the early hours of the morning before sunrise.

She healed a previous injury in my pelvis due to childbirth. I have received lots of healing from the other side but never experienced immediate physical healing until being in this lady's presence. She is a tall, black, and elegant lady who is strikingly beautiful. Her presence feels comforting, strong, but gentle and loving. As soon as I see her, I know I'm in safe hands.

When I was initially visited by her, she wore a red, brown and yellow tribal attire, but now she wears a simple white gown/robe with no grandeur. No airs, no graces, stripped back to her true essence. I asked her why she was dressed like this and she replied, "We have no need for material items, but it is easier for you to see us like this and it makes it less complicated for you to process. We wear nothing but appear to you how you can accept it.

Suddenly, I feel this beautiful warmth cradling

the left side of my body. My body feels weightless as though I am floating in nothingness. I want to sleep and stay here forever. My whole being feels blissful, no pain and no racing mind, just a sensation of stillness. The beauty and calmness of nothingness.

I feel her draw close as she identifies I am eager to escape my physical body and return to my real home. She gently draws my spirit back into my physical body as she grounds me and brings my conscious mind gently back into the moment. I feel so loved, protected and understood. I feel safe as though cradled in this sacred space.

Tears roam freely down my face as I can't control the deep loving contentment inside. I feel only love and happiness. I tell her I'd like to work on healing others when I return home (by this I mean when I die!). I want to work as part of one of these teams' helping humans and not be reincarnated.

I'm told, "Jane you have an important job, for the words you use will heal millions. You will heal others but first, we must heal you. The healing will continue and will be completed exactly at the right time. You have earned the right to open this door. Well done. It is now time to go back." Before I know it, I'm back surrounded by my healing team. What has just happened?

Where and what is all this leading to? I need time

to process all of this. I remind myself to remain focused, to check if I am fully cleansed before I return to the material world. Once returned to the material world, I contact the lady I have been healing and check if she is okay. I arrange another date and time in two weeks to do another healing.

I know there is no more I can do for this lady; everything has been completed. I need to double-check if everything has been removed and we have completed all we can do to help this lady move forwards on her journey. I must explain to any other healers out there a mistake that I made in the early days of doing . . . Let's call it more extreme healing methods.

I initially didn't know the proper cleansing methods, until eventually, I was shown by my healing team how to be cleansed. It wasn't until I learnt the Shaman techniques, I had the ability to work in the correct dimension for me. It is so important after healing another that you disconnect from the person's energy.

I would follow all the exact procedures taught by well-known healing methods, but this was not, and is not enough. You must connect to your healers or source or whatever you believe in and feel comfortable working with. You must make time to connect, see, feel, sense, however you work and not simply imagine, but know you have been cleansed.

If you fully connect, they will have access to showing and teaching you the correct procedure for you. Every healer is different. When you connect properly, you will never doubt again, as you will see and physically feel a cleansing method and procedure. This is not imagination; this is very real.

Imagination is not good enough; you should be able to work at a level where you have no doubt that your whole being has been cleansed. If you can't do this then perhaps, ask yourself seriously why you would want someone else's energy infiltrating yours. Healing, as I have learnt the hard way, is a selfless, serious honour, not merely a certificate easily obtained.

Sorry, if I have offended anyone. This is purely said with kindness, so nobody becomes ill. Ultimately, the true teachers of healing are, whether you choose to believe or not, the spirit world, God, divine whatever label you choose, who work in love and light. Please don't kid yourselves. You only work in pure light/love for there is always an element of darkness as one cannot survive or exist without the other.

Complicated but true. Virtually most of my life, I have chosen to believe only in love and light. Throughout this book, you will discover as I did that, unfortunately both dark and light, yin and yang, good and bad, it all exists.

I DECIDED TO TAKE A BREAK

I've been invited to a sound bath, which I've never been to before, but I'm open-minded. One of the instructors is my Shaman teacher who is using the drums. So, if nothing else, I know the energy in the room will be cleansed properly. I'm looking forward to simply lying there, relaxing and who knows, I might fall asleep or drift off somewhere nice.

My spiritual development has been moving very quickly so I'm looking forward to some downtime. I turned up and we were invited into a medium-sized room where there were several mats laying in the room for each of us to lie upon. There are drums, a few brass bowls, rattles and something that looks like it is going to make the same sound as the old-fashioned triangle you used to play at school.

On the left side of the room are three enormous, beautifully polished, shiny gongs. We have blankets to keep us warm and the atmosphere feels calm as I check the energy. I'm pleased to discover it has been thoroughly cleansed. If a room is full of stagnant energy, it really is not conducive to someone like me and makes me feel irritated and on edge.

I noticed the room hasn't got any windows, which if I'm being honest, I don't like, but I'm instantly reassured by my guides that I was protected. As I laid there, I felt comfortable and warm as I allowed myself to sink into the floor. I'm going to enjoy this, let someone else do all the work and just listen and chill. Heaven! I was so relaxed I felt I was already slipping into a light trance.

We were taken through a meditation, walking through a magical forest. The trees were extremely tall. As you look up, you can see the light streaming through the gaps and feel the warmth of the sun upon your skin. The forest is rich with an array of vibrant shades of green, shrubs, wild long grass and plantation.

You can hear the subtle sound of insects chatting amongst themselves and the faint sound of birds singing. I take in a deep breath as I feel every fibre in my body relax and sink gently into the floor as though I am encased in a gentle hug. We are taken through a gate to meet our spiritual animal, one that we currently need at this time.

I see a beautiful, white horse, with a silky, almost shimmering coat, who comes up close to my face. I notice its gentle, deep brown eyes, that have such depth, understanding and kindness in them. I'm fixated on this magical horse's energy as it feels so pure and innocent, yet strong and powerful.

As I'm stroking the horse, my hand is guided to touch between the horse's eyes. As I'm gently touching the horse, I can feel and see a hardened grey and earthy-coloured horn. Every time I touch the horn, I'm given insight and images of the true capabilities of this mystical creature. I'm shown images of the horse being able to fly and the ability to heal on touch.

As soon as my hand moves away from the horn, it disappears as though it never existed. Yet each time I touch this area, it appears again. Intrigued, I ask why this is happening. I'm told this is because I can see further into the distance and realms more than others. Each time I touch this horse's forehead, my forehead feels as though something or someone is physically touching, clearing and cleansing my third eye area.

I understand this sounds farfetched, but it's as if something is activating my third eye, forehead area. My forehead feels lighter, freer, and how it should have been all along. I then see the animal fly. I now have to discipline my mind, for I'm starting to question the reality of all of this and whether I am just making all of this up.

I quickly decide to remove the logical and analytical side of my brain and return into a light trance and back into this very moment. The meditation journey continues where we are taken to a specific place surrounded by crystal formations, and lay down where we are to meet our shaman partners.

I feel even more relaxed as I hear the drums beating in the background. The sound of the drums is blissful for it fills my soul with contentment, familiarity, happiness and pure love. I'm in my familiar territory, which makes me feel strong, powerful, and protected. I hunger to stay with my tribe forever, but yet I'm fully aware I still have so much more to do in this lifetime.

One day, I will have a choice to remain, but not now. As I'm lying there, I notice several faces appear, I recognise them all from past previous family lives. I stop myself from prying as I remind myself, I'm not here to work by gathering information as a medium does, but to remain neutral in the moment and perhaps allow myself to receive.

It fascinates me when I'm connected to the shaman world, I can see everything so clearly but when I work in the higher realms, I'm not permitted to fully see their faces or perhaps identity. I'm allowed to fully see some of my healing team but not all. Why? I'm sure I'll find out when they think I'm ready.

Within the meditation, as I lay there, I feel, sense, smell and see smoke being blown into my forehead as though once again, the third eye is being cleansed and purified. I'm so relaxed and comfortable being within this space. As I'm bathing in the moment, I then see my intestines, yes intestines, being removed from my body and being played with.

I'm watching as though this is completely normal and fascinated by the process. I'm shown a nick, damaged tissue which looks angry and inflamed. A shaman proceeds to use what looks like some sort of needle and thread and starts to repair the damaged tissues. I'm instantly shown blood dripping from my wrist into a bowl.

As I'm observing, my spiritual body elevates up and slightly out of my body to drink the blood from the bowl. I'm being told the reason I am tired all the time is because my intestines are not able to absorb the iron from my diet properly. Wow! Fascinating, that would make perfect sense and explain some of my symptoms.

I remind myself to stop thinking and remain in trance. Suddenly, the vibration in the room changes, I feel cold and can feel my physical body trying to adapt to the shift. Throughout this change, I feel an eerie calmness and a sensation of nothingness. What do I mean by nothingness?

When you are in the presence of divine, sacred healers, you feel so loved, comforted, safe, and blissfully happy, you could cry. When for example, you might be visited in the night by an intrigued spirit who is interested in your energy, you initially get a fright. When you are in the presence of something that feels dark, evil and threatening in this world or another, you feel physically nauseous, repulsed and want to run away from the situation.

I presume these beings, although very powerful, are a unique mixture of a bit of everything. A perfect species of light and dark, that's how it feels. I'm not scared, worried, or frightened, but I can't say I feel pleasure or enlightenment by being near them. I genuinely feel an unusual sensation of nothingness.

I also know these beings have nothing to do with shamanism and work on a higher frequency. I can't fully see them, but they feel incredibly tall, taller than the room, and are wearing black robes with a form of headdress which looks like an old-fashioned top hat. They are gathered around me as though discussing the next move for healing or my progression.

I hear very clearly a baby crying as though it is in the room. Yikes! No! They are enhancing my hearing. I can feel a frequency in my ear being adjusted. This is the one thing I'm not comfortable with. Interesting I suppose, I'm trying to convince myself this is fine. The gongs are played by one of the teachers, it's awful. I was expecting this to be enjoyable and find myself hating it.

The frequency is unbearable as though every ounce in my body is fighting against the frequency of this horrendous noise. I want to physically get up and run out of the room, but I'm intrigued as to why my body is so repulsed by the sound, surely it can't kill me. "Jane, man up and get on with it!" I forbid myself to escape the perils of this room.

As I lie there, I can feel the vibration of the gongs shudder and shake against the left side of my head, especially the eye, as though trying to dislodge something within my skull. I can feel my body putting up a good fight to retain whatever it is within the left side of my head and specifically the eye.

I'm pleading with myself to let go of this darn thing that has caused me so much unease, ill health and lack of equilibrium throughout my body. Please just go! The gongs get louder and louder as though trying to help the process of dislodging this foreign thing within the left side of my brain/eye.

I want to scream as the pain is horrendous, I'm feeling faint. I can feel the colour draining from my body and desperately trying not to retch. In my head, I kept repeating, Please, please, please, get rid of it! I give you permission to clear the crud, energy that I no longer need, now!" It feels like it's being dislodged and starting to break away. I'm scared, my brain feels like it is going to shatter into a million pieces.

My head feels gigantic as though it is filling the entire space of the room, beyond human capacity, and yet I continue to feel calm as I'm feeding off the energy of the surrounding tall, dark beings. They are filling the surrounding area around me with a sense of nothingness that allows me to remain calm. How can this be? I know for sure without these beings I'm ashamed to say, I feel I would have crumbled.

I don't know to what extent, but I know it would be physically dangerous. I'm feeling tired, beaten down and begging, please just free me from this thing! The gongs slow down. I feel a mixture of relief but then annoyance as I was so close to being free from this thing within my head. I know there has been a shift, but in what? I will find out once the procedure has settled. That was so intense and a little unsettling, yet I know I'm one hundred percent protected.

I will make a full recovery, but as I'm fully aware at exactly the right time. Bloody hell, that was hideous! I have a little chuckle to myself, searching for a positive. "Well Jane, it could have been worse, I could have projected vomit on the surrounding people!" I have come to the realisation and reluctant acceptance that there is a more powerful source controlling an element of my journey.

Finally, I hear the comforting, familiar and earthy drumming which I love. The sound of the drums fills my body with warmth, safety and peace. Funny really, how I was so reluctant to participate initially with any form of shamanism, but now it has become a comfort blanket which fills me with joy. Just shows how many potential pleasures in life we could be missing out on, due to the beliefs often we are born into, including the many fears we are taught.

It's so important that we challenge or at least reflect and expand our often indoctrinated upbringings. Perhaps, for those that don't want to question as they are happy with what they have been taught, that's also fine, for those who judge others, stop! Maybe instead of judging, allow freedom and admiration for those who want to explore.

It's 2023, a year finally to get a step closer to accepting all our wonderful differences and allowing all, one day to live in peace and harmony. Gosh, that was hippified! Life can be so much easier if we stay in our comfort zones, but I question why are we here, what for? I have suspicions that the reason is, we are here to learn as much as we can through experiences, not simply reading and studying other people's perceived views.

Of course, I could be wrong, yet I very much doubt it, with what I have witnessed. I have been taught from birth through my religious upbringing that there is no such thing as reincarnation. Yes, once again this lifetime would be much less complicated to adhere to the rules. For years I had seen and witnessed evidence that reincarnation does exist, but chose to not accept it for at the time,

I simply couldn't process it and if I'm being totally honest, hated the thought or possibility of having to live another life. No, thank you! The truth is, certain beliefs are correct. The reality is everyone can believe whatever they want and that it is not for any of us to judge. Live as good and kind a life as you can, never intentionally hurt another with words or actions and we will all be fine.

If you have done unkind things, don't worry, for there is plenty of time to put love and light back into the world. It's never too late to change! Sorry, I deviated again! Back to sound and meditation class. The drumming slows down as we return from our meditative state back into the here and now. Thank goodness for that!

The lady who was playing the gongs commented

on the intensity and high frequency of the gongs as though the gongs were synchronising trying to balance someone within the room. No shit, Sherlock! That will be my brain. "Oh the joys of being me," I thought. I'll keep that one to myself.

The final part of the sound meditation is when we all go around the room to discuss what each one of us experienced. I'm not a fan of this part, as frankly, while working in mediumship, we deal with facts and evidence. So this part could be made up of mumbo jumbo. How rude of me, but I have an analytical mind, sorry. Everyone had enlightened and relaxing journeys so as it became nearer to my turn, I decided to summarise.

I felt a little amused that I had admitted to basically seeing some sort of unicorn and how it was clearing and activating my third eye. I then casually mentioned there were loads of higher beings in the room. I then pointed to another lady in the room and explained these are beings you also work with. The lady looked a little surprised and then confirmed she knew what I was talking about.

The lady playing the gongs looked amused and commented how relaxed and unbothered throughout the session I appeared. I assured her this was my normal, without going into detail. The shaman lady who was playing the drums confirmed to the other lady this was perfectly normal for me and one of the ways in which I worked. I found it interesting how two sound meditation teachers were so different.

One was more spiritually advanced, the shaman teacher. She found it perfectly fine, whereas the other lady looked bemused. I had a little giggle to myself and thought if only you both knew the whole story. As I looked around the room, all the people were good, kind and very open-minded. It's healthy to be open-minded, but I also think it is healthy to question and decide for yourself.

It had been an interesting experience, but I knew and felt I didn't belong amongst these people. We all have different paths. I'm not here to play at this for I'm here to push forwards and work in the chosen field the spirit world wants me to do. I hope and feel my chosen path is to help heal others.

Sometimes I think, "What is wrong with me? Why can't I just simply bathe in the beautiful sounds and embrace the experience like other people?" The reality is that I sense there is urgency on the other side to get me up and working as we all know, we are not here very long. I can feel the drive in the spirit world for it is relentless.

Once I have mastered one aspect of a healing technique, I'm pushed onto another. That's just the way it works, at the moment! I also identify that there is no other teacher that can develop me other than the pure source, spirit world, whatever you wish to call it. The funny thing is I also know, we already have the answers within us, just not always self-confidence.

So, would I go again to these sound baths? Yes, but only when guided to, so I can gain or learn something from my guides. I still enjoy attending spiritual workshops occasionally, as it's always nice to meet other like minded people.

IT SEEMS, THERE WAS A PURPOSE TO THE SOUND BATH

After that sound bath, my lucid dreaming increased beyond belief. I'm experiencing what feels like flashbacks from perhaps previous lives. It's like the excruciating pitch and sound of the gongs has woken up something previously trapped within my memories. The themes once again are all military based.

I'm being used in an undercover evil and corrupt warfare. I can hear the words of my friend Becky suggesting that in a previous time/space/life, I would have been used as a super soldier to do and perhaps, be part of some sort of government/military corruption or perhaps, I hope good.

I can't fully process Becky's opinion on this as there isn't enough evidence, but I must admit some of what she has said would correspond with these awful dreams. This is one of my delightful lucid dreams - short, sweet and disturbing. I can't stress enough that lucid dreaming is so real it feels more real than the here and now.

You can see, sense, feel, smell and with

perseverance, in time, control certain elements. Here goes, I'm an undercover female attached to the special forces. I'm carrying what looks like a shopping bag, close within my arms, as though my life depends on it. I keep checking to see if nobody can identify what I'm carrying and the blankets within are not hindering the baby from breathing.

The baby looks poorly, grey, and his breathing is shallow. I must get this child out of harm's way to people who can help him. The child is sacred, the key to unravelling secret doors. This child must live, because it is vital for humanity. The military training kicks in, all emotions put to the side.

There must be no vulnerability exposed as I could endanger the mission and the life of others. I'm blending into society, looking cool, calm and relaxed whilst simply holding what could be perceived as shopping. I desperately need to get back to the set location where I can hand over this special baby.

I have a constant pitted feeling within my stomach for the heightened state of alert is physically taking a toll on my body. I remind myself, discipline, lives are at risk. What we are dealing with, it is not only corrupt but evil. As I'm walking through a car park, I'm scanning the surroundings for any threats.

There is a man in his car shouting over to another gentleman, asking if he would like his parking ticket as it still has over an hour on it. The man declines as he is about to leave. The man in the car turns and directly looks at me offering me the ticket. Within a split second, I decided to accept the ticket so as not to draw any prolonged attention.

I walked over to the car and just as I'm about to reach forward to accept the ticket, I immediately noticed that the male driver and female passenger were elite and scientifically-modified soldiers. They both have athletic builds, fair hair with piercing blue eyes. As I heard them laughing at me, I noticed their skin was red as though sunburned and the freckles and pigmentation beneath the surface of their skin was visibly exposed.

It's as though they have been put through some sort of intense ultraviolet light therapy with a radioactive substance. Their laugh was eerie as though they had completed their mission of getting near enough to me and this sacred child, to destroy us. I'm for a brief second startled, frozen in time, as I dropped the ticket.

Professional training kicks in, I'm running darting in and out of parked cars. I can no longer see them, but I can hear the echo of their sinister laugh. Are they radioactive and if they were, with what substance? Has the substance used on them infiltrated me, worse the baby? I suspect it could have but I needed to stay calm and inform the team of the current situation.

What do I mean by my team? I'm part of some sort of organisation, but this time, an organisation fighting for justice and truth. A professional team consisting of others, predominantly ex-military personnel who have also escaped the evil, corruption of a hidden scientific, vile, unheard-of organisation, the public are not aware of.

Many of the members previously were unaware how and what they had been used for until experiencing disturbing flashbacks, dreams and memories came filtering through. Horrified by the deception and cruelty, they had perhaps inflicted on others. These super soldiers had no choice in their actions. They were handpicked, some chosen from birth.

Time to sit in silence or fight back. Time to protect others from the perils of pure evil and put an end to this. I recognise another member in the distance, I breathe a sigh of relief. This person now becomes my surveillance, my ears and eyes, so I can get to a specific location to pass on the intel.

Finally, I can message in the codes informing the enemy is near, dangerous and contaminated.

All members are to keep away from me as I'm potentially contaminated. The child has shallow breathing, unresponsive, but still alive. I know where I must go, which is a specific site for decontamination drills and procedures.

Panic is setting in as I know I have limited time, if there is any chance of this baby surviving. My heart is racing, I must do everything to protect this child! I suddenly wake up, no gradual awakening. It's as if I've been forbidden any further access to information. I can still feel the pitted, nauseous sensation in my stomach.

I can still vividly see the genetically modified soldiers and their piercing, strikingly, light blue eyes. I can distinctly hear that awful sound of dark, eerie laughter that I can't seem to eliminate from my mind. The horror of the damaged illuminated freckles exposed upon sunburned skin.

Chemicals manufactured and pumped throughout these soldiers as though their mere lives are of less value than lab rats. New and undiscovered technology being manipulated for what? One thing is for sure, not for the good of human life and the environment. I also know this dark organisation will stop at nothing to perfect a scientifically modified, advanced, powerful - both physically and intelligently, controlled super soldier.

How do I know this? I don't know, but I just do! As I lay there in bed feeling sadness and a strange grief sensation within my chest, I contemplated how many lives would have been destroyed or experimented on to get to this stage. Who and what is behind this evil, but more important, how could it be stopped?

I desperately want to believe this is merely a nightmare, yet every ounce in my body tells me differently. I want to compartmentalise and put this horrid, very real dream in a locked box never to be revealed again, but I can't. My gut feeling is screaming this is anything but a dream.

Lucid dreams are very real in the moment and always hold an important message or teach us to process an inner issue. Yet these disturbing super soldier dreams feel different. They feel like a flashback of such a familiar time that as much as you try to question and rationalise the situation, you know deep within, there is truth in what you are witnessing.

I also know I can't become consumed with this information, for firstly, who could you share this with and secondly, I can't prove any of this is true. But I know there are others out there having these same flashbacks, waking up frightened and covered in sweat. Perhaps in the future this will all come to light, as I believe in the truth.

Truth cannot be stifled and always eventually rises to the surface. Blimey, imagine the reaction to this one! After a couple of days of trying to console myself with there is nothing I can do and then reminding myself how positive and grateful I am with life, I decide I need answers.

I don't want to ask my guides for the truth, but I can't process how very real all of this crazy super soldier stuff is. I need to know one way or another, what the hell are all these dreams, flashbacks about. I ask why I'm shown such upsetting and frightening scenes. I even result in saying, "I can't do this anymore. No more, I've had enough!"

The answer I get from the spirit world is, "Jane, don't over analyse, just write! We need you to stay focused and write. The words you write will help others understand and realise that they, like you, are not alone." Well, that's great, perhaps it's better for now, I don't know anymore. I must stay focused and finish this book and then perhaps, I will be free of these nightmares.

Whilst writing this part, the penny drops. One of the things from the previous dream was a constant nagging within and a concern for that poor baby. Did the baby survive? I'm told by my spirit team, the baby indeed did and that's why they allowed me to hear a baby cry in the sound meditation.

Very clever, the spirit world! Some could argue, what a load of bollocks! Yes, perhaps but I need to believe that sacred baby survived. Hopefully, for the good of humanity. Yikes, that's deep!

BACK IN THE REAL WORLD

As I continue to write this book 'The Reluctant Medium Part 3, I have just released 'The Reluctant Medium Part 2.' I thought I had become more accepting of sharing my truth, yet my body feels on heightened edge, and I feel quite anxious. Gosh, I wish I could just get over this childlike fear and vulnerability.

I compartmentalise and then rationalise the fact that nobody knows who I am. So why so much anxiety? Over the years, I have learnt a technique to step out of the moment and watch how I am behaving. It's a great technique as once you can see how you are behaving, it enables you to defuse or certainly reduce the overreaction to everyday things in life.

The problem is, I have this imminent feeling that things are about to change whether that be physically, spiritually or materialistically. Change is present in the air which feels a little unsettling, so I remind myself change is positive, exciting and good. I like to look at more challenging times as lessons in the hope that one day, I will be able to resonate and understand more people along the path.

Don't get me wrong, I don't always feel like this when I'm in the thick of it, mostly when I'm further down the line and can step out of the current situation and reflect. So, am I happy I have experienced PPPD (persistent, postural-perceptual dizziness)? Strangely, yes, for I'm a more understanding and compassionate person towards other medical conditions, I literally never gave any thought or consideration for.

Surely my change in thinking is a good thing. We rarely give any thought of others hardships until we have fallen into depths of despair ourselves. I'm honestly thankful for everything I have experienced, especially the hardships as it has made me who I am today. Basically, a nicer person.

I've come to the realisation that maybe, I will never be fully comfortable sharing my journey but that is okay. We are all different and that is a good thing. Imagine a world where we were all the same and believed in the same views. I'm bored already, sounds to me like engineered thinking and robotic.

As humans, we must not allow robotic thinking and behaviour ever to become normal, as much as some perhaps darker thinking people would perhaps like. Human flaws are not only endearing, but keep us humble and real.

LIFE IS GOOD

Through trial and error, I have created a method that helps me get physically through the day. As I have discussed previously which I'm not going to harp on about, I still struggle (due to my PPPD), with sensory issues with the demands of this busy world. Too much noise, bright light, and moving objects fatigues my brain.

Each day, usually at 2pm, I go and have a lie down. I go into a meditative/ trance state and receive healing. Sometimes, I just sleep to recharge my mind. If I try to push through the day without a rest, I feel nauseous, off-balance and so tired I can slur my words. As much as it frustrates me, it allows me to fit back into the world and function like everyone else.

This is another thing I don't share openly, as I don't want to come across as lazy or weak. Would I think of another person like this? No, but I have an unhealthy relationship with myself being seen as weak. I know this is wrong, but that's how I honestly feel. Anyway, as I'm having a lie down, nothing exciting or new, my jaw starts to be manipulated and put in an end range position.

I'm so used to this type of physical healing, I'm

not perturbed in the slightest. It all settles down as I feel myself start to fall gently into sleep. I'm so peaceful and relaxed, when all of a sudden, my head is forced into an elevated, twisted position and my jaw on the left side is lifted out of what feels like the socket and is aggressively repositioned.

The facial muscle tissues made a tearing sound, as I could physically feel an almost ripping sensation down the left side of my face and the side of my head. I lay, frightened to move, as everything returned to normal and the sensation in the room felt so calm. I cautiously and slowly moved and quickly realised no lasting damage had occurred.

How could this be? I also knew the healing spirit team that surrounded me worked with such precision and expertise that I'm in safe hands. So, the question is, would I allow a human to treat me like this? Not a hope in hell! I have been treated by the best over the years for numerous injuries and have never witnessed such precision and intelligence.

Not to forget as humans, we all make mistakes, but through choice not with my neck and brain. No thank you. The next few days, I've noticed I feel more alive. I have more energy and my eyesight and balance feels more stable. I continue to lie down as I'm fully aware I'm not completely over the finish line. Nevertheless, I have a joyous feeling that I'm getting closer.

The healing sessions still sporadically continue for the spirit healing team haven't fully fine tuned me. What do I mean by this? Basically, in simple terms whether you are aware or not, or want to believe or not, we have different energetic layers around our physical body. Not to forget energetic layers within our body.

My team is balancing my physical, spiritual and energetic layers to perfection so when I'm working in the future, I will no longer feel off-balance or suffer from ill-health or fatigue whilst working in higher frequency/vibrations. Bloody hell, wouldn't that be wonderful! Completion and perfection, balance within, for me, a dream come true.

The ability to work with my spirit team with no adverse side effects and to have the ability when given permission to work within other dimensions to help people. That really would be an honour and what I truly desire.

Well, that's what I have been told time and time again. "Patience Jane. Trust Jane. It has already occurred in the future." Gosh, I really hope so, I also know this to be true, but my goodness, it's been tough staying positive.

A DAY OF JOY

I love Thursdays. Every Thursday, I get to spend the day with my mum. We usually get whatever shopping we need and then spend time together chatting over a well-earned coffee, usually two. This Thursday, my mum needed to get back a little early as she was having a roofing job priced up.

The guy who was pricing the job was an old friend of my sister, who would frequently spend time with our family when we were growing up. I never really knew him as I was the younger sibling and was frequently told to go away, as siblings do. As we returned home, my father had already made him coffee and was chatting away in the kitchen, literally like old times.

We all had a good laugh reminiscing over old times and finding out the usual, how many kids he has and how life had treated him over the years. As I was listening, I was toying with the idea for him to price up a job, as I needed my guttering replaced, but I was reluctant to ask.

I felt like I didn't want to get involved, yet my spirit team was pushing me to ask. Why were they pushing me? We continued to chat as he explained how busy he was with work and literally couldn't fit any more work in. I casually mentioned my guttering needed fixing and perhaps in the future if he was free, he could book me in.

"Right, I've done my bit. So stop pushing me to ask," I thought in my head. I suddenly realised the time and how I needed to get back for my daily rest, so I could function when the kids got home from school. As I said goodbye and mentioned how lovely it was to see him again, he stood up and said he also needed to go.

As I'm walking to my car, he comes over and says, "Jane, you only live around the corner so if it's okay with you, I'll come and have a look at your guttering?" I told him that would be really kind and I would appreciate that. Yet I felt reluctant to, my throat constricts as though I'm being firmly told, just get on with it.

Before we know it, I'm back home and he is already up the ladder looking at my guttering. I have a little chuckle to myself at how fascinating life is. I was having coffee this morning with my mum and now I'm chatting to an old family friend that I haven't thought of or seen for over thirty years.

As we are chatting away, he asks me if I'm still working in the fitness industry. Out of nowhere, I tell him I'm a writer, which horrifies me, as I know what the next question is and really don't want that conversation. Bingo! I guessed right. "Now get yourself out of this one, Jane." I think to myself.

He asked intrigued, "Jane, what is it you're writing about?" There was a silence for a moment as I thought carefully about how I should reply. "Nothing exciting, just spiritual stuff on nature, life, death, a bit like poetry." I spoke. "Tell me more, I'm into spiritual stuff, and used to see a healer," he said. Blimey, I didn't see that one coming!

So, we have a free and open conversation and I mention in a gentle manner a little bit about mediumship to see how open he is before telling him I've been practising shaman healing techniques and currently studying EFT (emotional freedom techniques) to see if that could help those who might need it.

I forgot to mention, this conversation is taking place outside the front of my house where nobody knows anything about, let's call it my creative side. Out of nowhere, he looks at me directly in the face and says, "Okay Jane, what would you say to me then?" My throat constricts as I feel my guides stepping in so closely, I have no option but to relay the information.

As you know, I don't share others' private messages, but I can tell you, his father, who had died, urgently needed to speak to him. I got to see clips of his childhood and what had occurred and how he felt so he could accept the information to be real. Basically, his father was incredibly proud of him and remorseful for not showing his true love whilst on earth.

The father asked for forgiveness. The power and control had been placed in the son's hands. The family friend looked at me and said it didn't matter whether he chose to forgive his father as he was dead, so it didn't make any difference. I looked him directly in the eyes, knowing full well my spiritual team had entered my energy.

I felt masculine and authoritative. I repeated, staring into his eyes as though into his soul and said again, "Do you forgive him? It's your choice, but he cannot progress on the other side. Do you forgive him?" The family friend just stood there, staring back into my eyes and nodded gently and whispered, "Yes." As he said this, his eyes began to fill with tears and then he said loudly and shocked, "Fucking hell, Jane, I just felt something move within me, I physically felt that, it was real."

He kept repeating the sentence as though he couldn't yet process what had just occurred. I quietly said to him, "You can begin to heal now." That was such a surreal moment, we were both locked in time where healing had happened in front of our very eyes. I saw what had shifted energetically and he had physically felt it.

He then turned around to me and said, "No more Jane, you are scaring me." I told him not to be scared and I wouldn't say or do anything else. I did say to him that us meeting today wasn't a coincidence as they don't exist. We both abruptly went into polite mode as though what occurred hadn't taken place which I went along with as I could see he was overcome emotionally.

As he drove away in his truck, I could see him sobbing. I also knew he was very open, would process what had taken place but more importantly, he could finally heal. I have a strong suspicion that in the future, he also would be working to help others in some form of spiritual method. He had the right energy to be a medium/healer.

Finally, as I walked through the front door, I felt elevated with a heightened euphoria of humbleness, honour and love. I said aloud, "It's times like this I love being me!" I felt exhausted as my energy returned to the present moment, a little off balance, but felt so thankful to have the honour to witness another person heal before my eyes.

I thanked the spirit world for choosing me, but also mentioned if they could hurry up with the process, I could be working harder for them.

That day as I lay in bed, I passed out with exhaustion until I heard the knock on the front door. The kids were back home. I always allow myself time to process these occurrences, but I'm also disciplined enough to know when enough is enough.

That situation was unusual for I was being used as a medium, but then channelling healing through to another. There was no conscious effort, it all flowed effortlessly as though once again, I had done this all before. I giggled, as it wasn't appropriate or professional to do this in the street. Yet it was so organic and was the right thing to do. I suppose you could argue this was irresponsible.

I must agree, as this doesn't normally happen, and I certainly wouldn't advocate ever working in this way, but that day it was vital. I would argue there is a higher force that has a superior intelligence, full of love, purity, and knows exactly the honourable and correct process.

Who are we to turn our back on an opportunity to help heal another? Thought-provoking if nothing else. Sometimes in life you must do the right thing even if it means breaking the rules.

DIDN'T SEE THIS ONE COMING

I'm so excited as I'm meeting up with two very good friends which I haven't seen for ages. We all live in different areas so are meeting up at a motorway service station in Newbury. I absolutely love these girls as they are both ex-service military wives and so down-to-earth, honest, loyal, trustworthy and a good laugh.

I hunger to be around people where I can speak, openly, without having to worry what words you choose to speak, in case you offend anyone. Today's society has become so politically correct and sensitive to words rather than the content and how the words are used and expressed.

We are fast becoming a species that must always think before we speak so as not to offend another. Although this is all very nice, we are losing the ability to share our wonderful and often colourful personalities. I love meeting different people, personalities, especially free speaking people.

I dread the day we all become Victorian or worse, robotic in our polite and conforming views. Sorry, a yawn just came on. How boring life could become, but even worse, I think people could grow tired of interacting and getting to know one another. Back to these lovely ladies. The other thing about these ladies is they know I'm a medium.

I don't even know if that is the best word to describe me anymore, but basically, they don't care, for they accept me for being me. I must admit they did know me for some time before I took the risk and confessed my hidden secret. They both found it a little amusing as that was the last thing they expected me to come out with, as apparently, I appear so normal.

What was more impressive was they never treated me any different, which I love them even more for. Finally, we all meet up, huge hugs, then most important part, get the round of coffees in. We are chatting about how the kids are getting on between laughing at the things that have been going wrong in our lives.

Speaking so freely, not having to pretend how wonderful life is and how perfect teenagers can be. It bores the hell out of me when you speak to other people who blurt out how amazing the child is, the marvellous grades and what university they are going to. Please parents, stop!

If you are humble enough to mention you are struggling with your child's behaviour, it's amazing the other person will also confess, teenagers are really hard work. By being a little more honest, you can share the burden, plus the conversation is more interesting. Just my opinion, unless you have a perfect child, of course.

Although I suspect a lot of so-called perfect children struggle with low mood or are anxious with the expectation of having to succeed for perhaps pushy parents or simply what they are led to believe is expected of them in society. Maybe perfect kids do exist?

The conversation becomes more serious as one of my friends admits one of her children is struggling to sleep in his own room and has resorted to sleeping in her room. She says she had tried everything and felt exhausted. This lady is a well-respected professional in her workplace and has the knowledge and expertise to be able to deal with the situation. On paper, this is the one woman who is perfect for the job and a person others would turn to.

As she is explaining all the theories and methods she has tried, I can suddenly see inside her son's bedroom. I interrupt as my throat constricts and describe Fergus's bedroom to be a small box room which is painted in the colour orange. I can see something that looks dark and unpleasant as though crawling up the wall.

The presence is in the right-hand side corner of the room, it's not presenting in human form.

It feels cold, eerie and incredibly frightening for anyone, let alone a young child. I can feel Fergus's fear is almost feeding and empowering the energy of this thing. Fergus is rightly scared as he can feel it has been watching him.

My friend confirms Fergus's room is small and painted orange. My other friend looks bemused and says, "how can you know that, Jane?" I replied, I don't know, I just know, it feels easy to do when I'm given permission. Please don't think I go around looking in other people's rooms, I don't." We all have a little chuckle.

The mother of Fergus has a scientific and analytical mind and looks confused and then starts to justify other professional methods that could help Fergus. I quietly tell her there is no one that can help Fergus, not even a professional counsellor for he is a sensitive, spiritual child, and what he sees and feels is true.

I won't lie, I'm feeling reluctant to get involved in this situation, but I also know morally, I can't leave a child with that horrid, dark energy in his room. I have absolutely no desire to work with dark energy, but I can't leave a child in perpetual fear. I ask my guides whether I have permission to get involved and I'm immediately told I must.

Bloody hell! They know I don't like anything creepy, frightening or frankly dark and evil. As I'm thinking this, I feel my guide's presence draw closer, eradicating any self-doubts and confirming as I already know I'm fully protected and can't be harmed. I look my friend in the eyes and say, "If you want my help to remove it, I will. But I need your permission and I also need Fergus's energetic approval."

I explain I will ask Fergus but in a way where his conscious mind won't be aware of it so we don't frighten him unnecessarily. He doesn't need to know the full extent as he will be able to feel the energetic change once it has occurred. I can see my friend's analytical mind going into overdrive, but she admits she is so tired of the lack of sleep, she is prepared to try anything.

I tell her to spend a little longer on her decision and to ring me in a couple of days, where I will explain what I will be doing, once I have full permission. "Bloody hell, I only came for a coffee and a lighthearted conversation, really!" I said. We all burst out laughing at how ridiculous our conversation must have sounded if anyone was earwigging.

Well, I didn't see that one coming today. The spirit world never stops fascinating me on how they engineer me to meet the right people at the right time who genuinely need help. I'm happy to work for the spirit world, divine energy, whatever you choose to call it, if it is for the ultimate good. I must admit if I'm being honest, the thought of working to remove dark energy fills me with dread yet not fear. When and how has this changed?

TIME TO INVESTIGATE

A week has passed before I speak to my friend about her decision. She is keen to go ahead as Fergus has not improved and is still too scared to sleep in his own room. I explain the first thing I must do is get Fergus's permission. If he refuses to allow me access to helping him, I will not proceed.

I do not treat anyone without their permission as this is morally wrong, especially with children and animals where their voice isn't always heard. However insistent an owner or guardian is, I believe it is always up to the individual. I will also not treat anyone without the permission of my spirit team, for time and time again they have proven they know what is best.

I have been denied permission to read for people, but so far, not when it comes to healing. Although I tend to find people find or come across me at the right time. I don't currently advertise what I can do as the spirit world is insistent on me writing. Maybe one day, but I'm in no rush to declare to the world what and who I am.

I rather like staying under the radar and

blending into society without drawing attention to myself. I also have children and one of them is mortified with the prospect of my truth coming out. I do remind her that I'm fifty years old and can't stay hidden forever. I totally understand her feelings, because would I be happy if my mother was a medium/healer?

Probably not, but I know I would want her to be her true self. I suppose I have used that as an argument to stay anonymous, always thinking about my family's feelings and needs, yet I suspect the truth is, I just can't be bothered with the ridicule. I also know it is wrong and a little cowardly, speaking for myself not another, to not accept and be my true self.

I have my suspicions that in this lifetime, I will fully embrace myself and all my unusual differences. Time will tell! Back to what is important - healing others. To date, I haven't had anyone refuse to let me help them where healing is concerned, yet I don't take it for granted or presume.

You can send all the healing in the world, but ultimately if the person chooses not to receive it, surely in time it will revert? We are all different, but I have strong views on not forcing healing upon another without their permission. What about a person in a coma? Again, you always ask their permission.

If a person is unable to articulate, or for an animal or perhaps a child too young to understand, I simply ask their subconscious. I can feel some minds are baffled by this. What do I mean to ask their subconscious? In very basic terms, I blend into that person's/animal's energy and ask for their permission.

How do I do this? I struggle to articulate as I've always just been able to. It isn't something I have been taught. It's more of a knowing, but from where? Maybe a previous life, perhaps my guides. I can't give you a definite answer, nor will I make it symbolically fit. I loathe the action of making things fit or more like making things up.

If you don't know, say you don't know. I have a theory that the reason people take the mick out of especially spiritual readings is because there are too many people out there talking in riddles and symbolic methods rather than straight talking. That is my theory on why psychic/mediums are taken the mick out of.

What is it they say, a few bad apples! Just to reassure you, there are so many good, kind, honourable and very gifted mediums/psychics out there, you just have to search for them. There are good and bad in every walk of life, especially in positions of authority. Don't get me started on that one!

I deviate, sorry. As a healer you should always ask permission whether that be in person or their subconscious energy. A real healer will know instantly if they are given access before continuing. Before I begin healing, I always connect with my spiritual guides to ask what methods are correct for the person.

When it is a child, I'm usually guided to blend in with the child's energy to work telepathically to find out why the child is struggling and how they feel. It's literally like I'm having a conversation with the child in the here and now. Children are usually funny as once they start to feel safe and open up, you can't stop them talking.

I must mention whilst in conversation, I always ask their permission if it is okay to tell their parents how they feel. This makes a huge difference if the child is willing as it can help the parent take control and heal the child themselves. The funny thing is with children, when I ask if I can tell their parents they are always so far, keen for me to relay their feelings.

I would go as far to say, relieved they can pass the responsibility to me. Usually, the child has kept their feelings hidden from their parents especially as they become older. A common issue that occurs is they can sense parents aren't getting on with one another which makes them feel vulnerable and another very common issue is, fear of a parent dying.

As adults, we think children are not listening to our conversations, but they are like little sponges absorbing not only our words but our worries and concerns. So, I speak to Fergus 's mum and tell her I'm going to speak to Fergus to find out how he is feeling and what is going on. I then explain I will go in and do a healing, but there are no set procedures, as I will be working with my healing guides.

I will inform her with what I find at the end. Fergus gives me permission to work with him. He is a very sweet, kind, little boy who is also sensitive in nature and very spiritually aware. I ask him why he won't sleep in his room. First, he says he doesn't like the colour and that it is too small.

I can feel a reluctance to tell me the real reason as I feel heightened fear surrounding his energy. "Why else don't you like your room, Fergus? I ask. Before he has a chance to answer, I can see in my mind's eye, a dark mass in one of the corners of his room like a thick treacle substance climbing up the wall. It's in the right-hand corner.

The presence feels cold, empty, and dare I say it, not human. It feels foreign and an energy I haven't come across before. I also see a small hole in the ceiling as though he is being watched.

Fergus replies, "I'm being watched, I can see eyes looking at me. There is something in the corner of my room that scares me. It feels scary, I don't know what it is, but it won't leave my room. I feel eyes watching me. My tummy feels sick, I just don't like it in my room. I want to be near my mum. I need to be with mum. I feel safe when I'm near mum."

As Fergus talks, I can feel all his heightened emotions, panic and fear. He too can sense spiritual energies, but can't make sense of it and I know from experience from my own childhood, it can be petrifying. We continue our conversation, as he opens up about what else is upsetting him.

I'm not about to reveal all of Fergus's problems, but I can mention he was having a hard time at school. He showed me a picture of a boy who was jealous of Fergus's happy home life who was bullying him which nobody knew about. He gave me plenty of information so I could inform his mum to put a stop to this.

As Fergus was talking more about school, I could sense he was struggling to hear the teacher and his eyes felt strained whilst looking at the classroom board. When I approached the subject, he mentioned he didn't want to wear glasses as he didn't want to be laughed at. Out of nowhere he starts talking about Ellie who had died. (I later found out the name was Nelly!).

Nelly was the family dog who had died a few years ago but this had really affected him. Fergus, although only young at the time, would have felt all the emotions, sadness and grief of others so strongly. As I have already mentioned Fergus is sensitive and a gifted boy who feels deeply.

A family member had been having concerns with their health and Fergus had picked up on this which resulted in his fear of death. He also mentioned another family member who was always moaning about being ill, aches and pains. In his mind this became a huge worry for what and how was he going to survive if all the people he truly loved left him.

There was only one thing he could do and that was sleep by his parents to ensure they didn't die. If he slept near his parents, especially his mum, they would be safe and more importantly, he could keep an eye on the situation. Fergus had taken on the responsibility of protecting and keeping his loved ones safe.

More importantly, he could not stay in that awful bedroom with that scary black thing watching him. I then asked him if he would be happy for me to do some healing on him and then if it was okay for me to have a look at this black thing and see if I could remove it. He very gently and quietly replied with a sigh, "Yes."

I come out of the psychic/telepathic energy and start to go into a light trance whilst sending out my intention to heal Fergus with my sacred and divine healers, now! These aren't the exact words, but what you might notice is I'm direct. When working with the spirit world, you need to be precise, not wishy-washy so you get the correct results.

This isn't being rude, it just ensures both you and your team are synchronised. As I connect, I immediately feel any self-induced pressure fade away. Instantly, I am part of a process more powerful, clever, healing, and loving than simply myself. As I visualise looking at Fergus, they draw me to his third eye which is overactive.

The poor child is so sensitive, he is literally sensing and feeling an overload of spiritual and sensory activity. With my team, we calm down the third eye. The third eye is on the forehead between the eyes. By calming down this area, Fergus will become less sensitive to his own spiritual gifts until he is ready to use them.

Fergus will become more relaxed, less fatigued, and his journey in the material world will become more enjoyable. In time, if Fergus wants to use his gifts later on in life, he can. It is his choice. I don't believe, I know, there are lots of children who are very spiritually gifted, but suffering in silence and fear as they don't know how to control their gifts or feel scared or silly to talk about their experiences.

Some children are so young they can't articulate their feelings, resulting in perpetual fear and nightmares. When their parents take them to the doctors, they will be given very little help or maybe medication. For some children, this may be the correct treatment, but for most I suspect not! When will this conversation come to light? One size does not fit all.

How many people are taking medication due to heightened anxiety or seeing things in other dimensions, which they probably haven't dare to mention. Again, medical professionals should always be consulted first, but I repeat, one size does not fit all. I reiterate, always seek professional medical advice as there could be an underlying serious medical condition!

My eyes are instantly taken to different locations throughout his body, mostly energetic imbalances which relate to how Fergus is feeling, which will be relayed to his mum. For such a young child he has created a lot of fear and guilt within his body which presents as small shadows.

With precision, these dark shadow substances are gently removed allowing the whole person the freedom to heal. With Fergus, the shadows are removed via a surgical, metal, tube-shaped device that carefully sucks out the shadow. The shadow is then almost filtered through a small swirl of air and taken to another dimension. Did I just admit to that!

The area must be protected, usually using a grey clay substance as though patching up a hole. The area is then covered in a blue substance which calms and when used on a physical injury, reduces all inflammation. Finally, gold-loving and healing light. Each healing is completely different, no two people are treated the same as all individuals are unique.

It literally blows my mind once I come out of the energy and allowed to digest what has taken place. The spirit world really is superior to mankind. It's as though we are still working in the dark ages! The healing continues but this time the energy shifts telling me we are working on the physical body.

What do I mean? I mean there is a physical, biological irritation or injury that needs healing, it is real in this world. An injury or irritation the person will generally, although not always, know about. An example of this would be someone who experiences pain or discomfort in their digestive system or constant nagging pain in a knee.

I always know as the vibration feels more serious, total submersion in the moment and full concentration. As I go a little deeper in trance, I'm taken to an area of Fergus' body which is inflamed, looks angry, and one part looks sore and red. I'm told this is due to the overuse of antibiotics.

We go in very gently first, adding the blue substance to calm down the area. There is a tiny irritation and scar-like tissue causing, not a blockage, but not allowing the body to flow properly. One of my guides who works as a surgeon repairs the damaged tissue, as I watch in fascination and remain in the energy that he needs me to hold.

The work is complete, the area calmed, healed and protected. The energy returns a little lighter and not quite as serious. We check over Fergus and he is completed. I feel myself start to relax. No! The energy has shifted, I can feel Medicine man step in closer to my energy.

I should explain, Medicine man, or so I call him, is a medicine man from an African tribe (Shaman) who not only has the ability to heal, but has the gift of removing dark energies and cleansing spaces. I'm taken remotely into Fergus's bedroom; it feels cold, eerie and unwelcoming.

I must explain what I mean by "remotely". Remotely means you can be in a certain place, but have the ability to see in another place, for example, another part of the country or even overseas. I only use this method when I'm given permission by my spiritual guides, usually during a healing session.

You might have guessed, I would rather stick to working purely in love and light, but as I'm rapidly discovering you need to remove darkness so light can filter through. I can see clearly in my mind's eye the dark substance as though it senses our presence clinging on stronger to the wall. My body starts to do this swirling motion as though I am the Medicine man.

I feel powerful, courageous and fearless. I feel so tall, larger than the room, as though I'm engulfing the energy in the room. I have never felt so certain and confident of my ability to remove this dark thing as though I have done this several times before. I'm physically standing up in a slightly crouched position as my arms are held to the side as though about to pounce or gather the trapped energy like a cornered rat.

I'm swirling, physically and internally as I feel the swirl of energy deep within my body. The sensation is filling my body with euphoria and such strength and power. The dark energy is putting up a good fight as it is refusing to be removed. I take a deep breath before the swirling sensation ramps up a gear. This time, I can sense we are winning the battle.

I am going a little deeper into trance. The next thing I remember is the room returns to normal. The room feels calm, relaxed and pleasant. The dark energy has completely vanished. I instinctively know we need to check the whole house. We scan the house which feels riddled with a sordid, dark energy.

There is no specific entity, spirit, or alien thing. It just feels sleazy, dirty and sordid. I'm standing upstairs in my friend's house remotely (remotely means I'm not physically there but I can see inside her house from my home. Creepy, perhaps) on the landing, swirling as though we are sucking the energy from within the walls out of the building.

This process seems to go on forever. Finally, there is nothingness, calmness, normality. I hear the word, "Enough." I am not permitted to do any more. I have no scientific evidence, but I know the people who lived there before my friend moved in were struggling with life. A broken mixed family with one unpleasant character with a substance problem.

I sensed and could smell alcohol, yet it all felt sexual and sordid. The dark energy thing in Fergus' bedroom was feeding the current owners and the previous owners were feeding the energy of the dark thing. Blimey! I didn't see that one coming! How am I going to relay all this information to my friend? My friend has a very scientific and analytical mind so probably won't choose to believe any of it. Probably a good thing.

I must reiterate as soon as I have done any form of spiritual work, I spend time going back to my space, dimension where I am surrounded by my healing guides and receive thorough cleansing, healing and protection. I have learnt the hard way; you cannot just visualise a quick cleanse. You have to submerge yourself properly in it. Time-consuming, yes, but worth it for your own health.

TRY EXPLAINING THAT ONE

After the house cleansing which I would usually run a mile from, my analytical mind starts to kick in. Why, how, and more whys. I decide obviously my spirit guides are ramping up my energy or purely showing me what I could be capable of. The one thing that amused me was I had absolutely no fear. This is a woman dare I admit who previously wasn't even keen on the dark. I know the explanation of this.

As a child from as young as I can remember, I hated and feared the dark due to the constant spirit visitors. I used to lie awake, frantically trying not to fall asleep so they would stay away. Very rarely did this work, through exhaustion I would eventually pass out. I would feel so joyous, safe, and blissfully happy when I woke to the sight of the first rays of morning sunlight shining through the curtains.

I would always take a huge breath and breathe a sigh of relief. As a child, it always felt such an accomplishment to survive what I perceived as the horrors of nighttime. Finally, I could breathe, relax and feel safe. That was my favourite time of day, the first glimpse of light. Light has always resembled comfort, safety and security.

Darkness, still to this day, doesn't bring me as much comfort. Pretty amusing for someone who has been chosen to work with spirit.

The conversation with Fergus's mum takes place. I ask her as she is my friend whether she wants me to flower it up or just come out with the truth. No surprise, the truth. So first I go into what has been upsetting Fergus which she finds interesting and a little sceptical as I would expect.

She confirms a lot of what I have picked up medically to be correct which I knew nothing of. She immediately knew of the boy bullying Fergus and had her suspicions. She hadn't reacted to it as Fergus seemed to be coping. I must explain about my analytical friend who likes a scientific explanation for everything.

Whether she believes it or not, she is very in tune spiritually and if she chose to listen more to her instincts could be phenomenal. I have told her this several times, but she insists on fighting her true gifts. I also know that she herself will be working in this unexplainable and illogical field herself, not for a few years yet.

When I explain Fergus fears death, again she is sceptical and not fully convinced. I explain to her I'm just the messenger and perhaps when he is ready, he will open up. We continue through Fergus's feelings and how he is feeling at school.

He has been struggling with his hearing and she wasn't aware that he hadn't been wearing his glasses.

As we continue our conversation, I have a little chuckle because I can sense her mind doing overtime trying to explain how I could know these things. I think to myself I have explained so many times how I work yet, she just can't accept it. Sometimes, I find this frustrating, but then I must remember, my normal isn't everyone else's. One day she will!

We continue chatting about how sensitive and spiritually aware Fergus is and how I have gently calmed down his third eye to make the material journey less frightening. Again, a sense of amusement, but an agreement on how sensitive he is. The list continues and confirmation is given on the physical aspects, and she agrees perhaps, too many antibiotics have irritated his body.

Now for the serious conversation, what is going on with Fergus's room. I tell her in detail my findings and what I did to remove the dark energy. Silence, my friend is trying to process the findings. It's as though she needs more time to work out if any of this is true. I respect her feelings for I don't know whether I would want to have heard straight talking and frank words. (By the way, I'm not as free speaking with most, unless I know they can handle it.)

Although my friend is not convinced, I'm told by my spiritual team that she needs to hear the truth, for in the future she will have to adapt to this. Baby steps, I suppose. I admit cautiously that the whole house felt dark and sordid, although Fergus's was by far the worse. Silence again, this time, I'm worried I might have been too honest and concerned I might have upset her.

She begins to open up. She explains her initial gut instincts when she first viewed the house. She found the initial homeowners very strange, cagey, and low in mood, with no spark or pleasantness and didn't like being in their presence. I asked her why she bought this house if it didn't feel quite right.

Basically, like many others that buy houses with unpleasant energy, due to cost, she also has a large family and needs the space. Makes perfectly logical sense in the material world, but folks, if you are in a financial position to choose, forget how luxurious, cheap or pretty it looks. Always go with your gut feeling and how the building feels.

If something doesn't feel right or your stomach area starts to feel nauseous for no apparent reason, please listen. You will be right! Energy is very real, previous energies of prior owners can remain. Unhappy marriages, divorces, sadness, anger, etc can remain. As so can the energy of happy and loving homes.

Trapped energy of spirit people, entities, and strange dark things with no names do exist although thank goodness, this is not as common. On a positive note, we have all walked into a family home full of love and laughter, felt very comfortable, at home and wanted to stay.

Likewise, we all know when we walk into a home and start clock-watching as the home or people aren't welcoming and you sense they don't really want you there. Every single one of us feels these sensations, just most of us tend to try and rationalise. We even tell ourselves how silly we are for feeling these emotions and thoughts. Well folks, you are not!

I continue to explain further methods I used without scaring her, before explaining how Fergus was feeling and how he felt there were eyes watching him. I then felt my throat constrict and told her she needed to check the loft. I could sense not only was it energetic, but very real in the present time.

I could also see a tiny hole in the ceiling as though Fergus's room was being spied on. I chose not to tell her this as I didn't want to unnecessarily scare her and there was no proof, maybe I had got this one wrong. I reiterated she needed to check the house just for peace of mind that there was no camera or devices of any kind left behind.

As I said these words, I reassured her I was probably being silly and overreacting to make her feel more comfortable and we both laughed and made a joke out of my craziness. "On a serious note, I've done as much as I'm allowed. The energy in your home feels better, Fergus's room is clear, although I think it will take some time for him to sleep in his room as he has had a very real, frightening experience."

I then asked if she could change rooms, but it was not an option so suggested at least repaint the room a different colour and try to build up gradually the time he spends in there. I had seen, felt and witnessed what Fergus had experienced and there was no way at his young age, I would happily sleep in there.

Spiritually aware children take time to feel comfortable and accepting of their gifts. Bloody hell, it took me into my thirties until I felt comfortable in my own skin. I missed out that bit to my friend as she was desperate for sleep. I told her there was no quick fix to Fergus going back to his room, but he would in time. The conversation ended, as I asked her to keep me updated with how Fergus got on.

My friend thanked me although I could sense she hadn't fully bought into the situation, but that's fine. I would rather someone was a little sceptical than believe in everything a person said, especially with no scientific evidence. The main thing is I just hoped that Fergus would feel more settled, content and happy throughout his journey. I knew what I had participated in with my spiritual healing guides would help him, I had no doubts.

AN ALARMED FRIEND

After a week or so, I keep getting telephone calls from Fergus's mum, which unfortunately I keep missing. She is persistent so I know she needs to speak to me urgently, as usually, she is very laid-back and chilled. I eventually get a window of opportunity to ring her back. Before I have time to speak, she blurts out, "Oh my god, Jane, you won't believe what has happened. Fergus has opened up to me out of the blue how worried he is about me dying.

He started asking questions about the Queen dying and then a floodgate was opened. Poor little thing. I had no idea how worried he was, he literally showed no signs." I had a huge smile of happiness on my face, as I told her that was fantastic news. Let me explain, not always, but more common than not, after I have had a telepathic conversation with a child, usually within a few days, the child starts to talk to their parents about what is concerning them, if they feel safe enough.

It's like it is now safe to talk, because they have already had the conversation with me, and it feels more comfortable or normal to speak the words aloud. Why is this? I don't fully know, but I suspect they just feel braver to express themselves. My friend seemed so shocked with the synchronisation of events; I could sense it's blowing her analytical mind.

The other amusing thing was my friend had discussed all the spiritual healing and findings with her husband. "Blimey, how did he take it all? I won't be allowed to come out to play with you anymore. You will be forbidden to frequent with your witchy friend." I said laughing. "Well, he took it all very seriously, we checked the loft together and found nothing but an old bin bag of teddy bears which was a little creepy. Then wait for it Jane, you won't believe it, a hole directly looking into Fergus's bedroom as though something had been removed!"

I immediately felt a shudder go down my spine as I knew a camera or something similar had been watching this room. I also knew, thank goodness, it was before my friend had moved in. Again, it felt dark and sordid. "I forgot to mention the camera bit to my husband. We couldn't find anything else so I'm sure everything is fine now." She spoke.

I reassured her that everything would be fine now. The problem with working the way I do is I have no scientific evidence. I had no doubt that whatever had taken place in that house, was child-related and it filled me with horror and sadness. I had to accept there was nothing I could do to help fix what had occurred. Emotionally, if I allowed this, it could disempower me. Perhaps, I could even spiral into a darker headspace, but this wasn't an option.

I'm naturally a person who wants to fix things. I couldn't completely fix this, for whatever had previously happened, had already taken place. I had to discipline, compartmentalise, and detach from the situation. Look at the positives and at least I knew the energy in my friend's house was clear for her and her family to create their own happy, loving energy. The cycle of dark energy within that house had finally been broken and could do no more harm.

A few days later, I received another telephone call from my friend. "Jane, you won't believe what has happened. I spoke to my husband and mentioned about the camera. He confessed he had found a camera when they first moved in, had put it in a drawer and forgot to mention it to me." she spoke. I then insisted she must get it out of the house. Anything to do with the energy of the prior owners must be removed as far away as possible from you all.

"Where is it now?" I asked. "My husband has still got it and was thinking about reporting what you had said to the police as he is now convinced something has gone on in the house." I started to nervously laugh and then spoke seriously. "You haven't got enough evidence; nobody will believe any of this, especially when you mention the word "medium." Just get rid of the camera and move on with your life.

I can't stress enough that you don't want that energy on the camera anywhere near you or your family." We both continued to make light of the situation and started to laugh about the prospect of involving the police. A few weeks later, I found out that my friend had heard a knock at the door from the previous owners looking for a delivery. There was no delivery and it all felt very odd. Thankfully, my friend's husband was at home.

The previous owner just stood there, as though waiting for something. My friend's husband still had possession of the camera as he was still in a moral dilemma on what he should do. He decided to hand the camera back to its original owner in the hope their paths would never meet again.

Creepy, it was as though the guy somehow knew his camera had been found, but refused to ask for it. Anyway, as I have said before, you shouldn't make things fit as there is still no concrete evidence. What does your gut instinct tell you? Thought-provoking if nothing else.

SOUL REMOVAL

Life continues with me dedicating my time to how spirit wants me to work, and that is writing. I've learnt the hard way by blatantly ignoring their wishes several times. However, I'm always brought back to where I need to be - writing! Really, of all the things! As I have mentioned before occasionally, I will be given permission to do healing, but literally only when it is engineered by them to come my way.

It amuses me how and when I'm contacted, as you never see it coming and it fascinates me how it literally falls my way. I find healing an honour and humbling to be given access and permission to work with my healing spiritual guides. The wealth of knowledge I'm submerged within is mind-blowing and truly a privilege.

An opportunity to help physically, mentally, or spiritually another person in great need, fills my soul with an unexplainable contentment and happiness. This is what I desire in the future to do more of, but as I'm regularly reminded, not until I've completed the writing. Whilst doing a healing for someone, towards the end, I feel my throat constricting.

I sense and feel there is something important my team needs to tell me. I know I must go back up to where I'm cleansed, but there is a sense of urgency. It feels very concerning, very serious. I detach from all emotions and continue to concentrate on the person that I have already finished healing. I still need to contact the person, give them an update on what occurred and if I need to do another healing.

As soon as I have finished speaking to the person, I immediately discipline my mind, no time to over analyse. I need to go to the dimension where I receive cleansing. As soon as I'm there, I'm immediately put through a funnel device that cleanses my energy, removing anything that does not belong to me. I suppose I should explain a little more what this funnel device looks and feels like.

It is how I have suggested a funnel of swirling wind that rotates rapidly around and within your body removing tiny particles of, I presume the person you have been healing. I have seen these particles in others that I've healed before. They look like tiny black pellets, blanks from a gun or a game of backgammon but smaller. These black spots can prevent people from healing.

They can be created within the person due to past experiences of trauma and self-loathing, fear, and guilt. Or unfortunately, by others. Believe what you wish as I appreciate there is no scientific evidence for my choice of words. Not yet! Anyway, this is only one example of what is removed as it varies from person to person.

Another example of what I have been given access to see is a transparent material/web substance, like a layer of clothing being removed from your body. I'm sure there are many things being filtered and removed out of my energy, but those are the examples of what I've been allowed to see. I've also been shown what the energy looks like once it is removed, which is a dark, treacle, sticky tar substance.

This substance is then removed via a swirl/funnel like a small tornado into a different dimension. I have never been shown the destination, it simply vanishes into thin air. My body, throughout my own cleansing procedure, feels relaxed, calm and light. Once the cleansing is complete, I'm allowed to walk out of the funnel as though opening a door to leave a room that is naked to the eye.

Back to the moment, as I come out, fully cleansed, I'm fully aware I'm surrounded by my spiritual healing team. The atmosphere feels different, serious whereas usually I'm greeted with happiness, blissful love and a sensation of celebration of our achievements in helping heal another. There is a sense of nothingness, but impending doom. It feels like I'm being sat down to be given some bad news, like a death is imminent.

I'm shown images and flashbacks of all super soldier memories. The images are extreme, fast and furious as they enter my vision. I shudder, feel nauseous, emotional and yell deep within my soul, "no more!" The images stopped, to my relief, for the flashbacks feel tainted, dark and evil. Every physical and physiological sensation deep within feels violated. I feel such a strong sensation of sadness, which turns into anger and rage.

I have this pitted feeling deep within my stomach of knowing I have been used, corrupted, and infiltrated for the gain of darkness and evil of others. A deep knowing I'm not clean, but tainted and dirty. I feel the strong closeness of my spirit guides surround me. Their presence fills me with strength and reassurance that I am not only fully loved, but protected.

It is then explained to me that in the future, if I choose, I will no longer receive any more super soldier flashbacks, unless there is a specific reason, but this comes at a price. The decision is mine to make and it involves me agreeing for a part of my soul to be removed. I'm initially baffled as in the Shaman world, we go in search to find lost soul parts to make the person whole, so they can continue their healing.

This goes against everything I thought I knew. I then ask if this will weaken my protection. I am assured that throughout the procedure and after, they will be able to fully protect me. I then ask whether I need to agree to this to complete my journey. I am told I will be a pure, light source for the spirit world to work through.

For me to complete my chosen journey, there can be no darkness attached to me. This is completely my choice; no other can help in my decision. What is my gut instinct telling me? What is every fibre, vein and cell shouting at me? What is Jane telling me? I already know the answer, for as bizarre as this sounds, my choice has already happened.

I agree for part of my soul to be removed. I'm feeling a little anxious and starting to question my decision, yet I know it is vital for moving forwards. A calmness and relaxation so gentle washes over and through my body. I feel the closeness and loving light radiate from my healing spirit guides infiltrate throughout my body.

I can see clearly through my mind's eye a see-through layer of material/substance being removed so lightly and gently away from the left side of my chest area. I presume this is the tainted, darkness and evil being removed from my soul. I feel physically no different, but I feel tearful, overcome with emotion of a mixture of sadness and relief.

All these feelings running through my veins that I can't articulate or understand for I don't know what they are. I say my goodbyes to the spiritual dimension and return to the here and now. That day, my eyes feel so heavy, tired as though I'm struggling to stay focused. I'm overcome with fatigue due to constant aching behind my eyes.

I need to go to bed, I feel strange, more physically unbalanced then normal and just need to retreat to the bedroom. I crave silence, stillness and nothingness. It's as though the new me needs to be repaired. Allow the physical, spiritual, emotional and mental bodies time to readjust. Within a matter of moments, I'm out cold, in a deep sleep.

I finally wake up wondering whether I have simply dreamed all of this. There can be no self-denial for I know deep within, it is my truth. Oh my gosh! What the hell! My mind starts to go into overdrive. I have a feeling of relief that I won't be pestered at night with disturbing military flashbacks, but then a little unsettled I agreed to have a part of my soul removed.

Will I never feel whole and complete? Have I done the right thing? What would the shaman community think of my irresponsible behaviour? Reality check, every single one of us is unique. What is right for one isn't right for another. Time moves on, so does healing, although too many choose to stay within limited boundaries.

If I had stayed within my comfort zone, I would still be using and believing in a healing method that does minimal to help another. As I'm thinking aloud, my guides draw in closely and I can feel them laughing in a supportive and reassuring way that everything is going to be absolutely fine.

I sigh with relief, for their loving presence, strength and protection reassures me I have made the right decision. The next few days, I still find myself revisiting the energy removal process. I question the logic and reality of it. The problem is as much as I'm searching for a rational explanation, there isn't one.

I know what I witnessed was real! It's time to have a harsh word with myself and accept some things can't be explained and move on. Something has shifted inside of my body. I feel more upright, balanced, and my eyes feel equal. What do I mean by this? For the last seven years I have been getting a constant eye ache/headache in my left side.

The discomfort has moved to both eyes, but

strangely feels more equal. I feel more balanced within my body. Not so much a fisherman on a boat at sea, a little, but more stable. Could this be the start of finally heading towards the finish line? I feel hopeful and a little excited at the prospect.

Since that energy removal (notice how I've changed the word soul to energy as I'm still a bit perturbed by the experience), I haven't had to date any more super soldier flashbacks, but I've been having images and reminders of past military experiences in this lifetime. I'm a person that once I complete a chapter in my life, for example, fourteen years in the military, I look forward and don't choose to reminisce.

The past is the past as some would say. The same as past sporting achievements. In my younger days, I was considered a talented footballer, but once the chapter came to an end, I don't discuss it unless it is brought up by a family member or someone who knows of my past.

To the point people are amused that I don't watch football as so much of my childhood was consumed by the sport. My feelings on this are, I'm a doer not a very good spectator. The chapter ended and I very rarely look back, same as my military days. I'm only interested in the here and now. What I can contribute in any small way, positively in the future.

The past is a part of my story, but certainly doesn't play a role in my future. Oh my gosh, I can feel a counsellor trying to label me with an up-and-coming fashionable condition. Whatever! That's how I am. Anyway, I'm experiencing lots of recurring memories throughout the daytime of my past military career. Things I haven't thought of for years.

In fourteen years, I served at eleven different bases. I gained a wealth of knowledge as it was a very busy and diverse time. I met a variety of characters and challenges along my way, which has made me the strong person I am today. The beauty of serving in the military is you learn very quickly, a variety of different personalities and how to play the game and ultimately survive.

I, under no circumstances, will reveal what went on in my military career. Some could argue perhaps, I've been indoctrinated. Perhaps, but I have a strong loyalty to my military roots. My gosh though, that time would make for good reading and horrify this generation of the lack of equality.

Hence it was at times awful, frightening, cruel and brutal. Not a place to express one's feelings and emotions. Weakness was not seen or tolerated. Oh, the good old days! Don't get me wrong, there were many fun times too and it certainly taught resilience, courage and determination.

I must admit I had some amazing experiences throughout my career, including spending the winter months teaching skiing in Germany, yet those joyful memories aren't appearing. All the memories are from more extreme and challenging times. I find this interesting, why am I revisiting these memories now, for I don't care for them.

It's like watching all these different parts of a puzzle blending with the super soldier flashbacks. It's like I need to process the past to free myself completely for future events. As though I'm being cleansed of all military traces. I'm not perturbed, more intrigued and fascinated to firstly, why and secondly, where is all this leading to.

Some of the military memories I find myself questioning, why I was even in certain locations. As I start to overanalyse, I'm scolded from my spiritual team that it is not my job to become consumed, just to continue my chosen path. "Write, Jane, just write!" Apparently, my journey will play a significant part in the future.

We'll see, I hope it helps others, still not fully convinced. I also came to my own conclusion. I haven't got the time, energy or desire to work out this complex puzzle for I know there are others already out there who have been chosen to seek, prove, and expose the truth. So, I let the memories continue to flow. I don't suppress them, just look at them as past teachings.

Some of the memories buried so deep within I thought I had completely forgotten. Once the memory resurfaced, it was crystal clear, every detail and person I had met, some of the faces I didn't know, and why and what I was I was speaking to them about. It felt like there were genuine blanks or periods of lost time.

Eventually, the memories subside which I find a relief as I've already explained I'm not a fan of visiting the past as I'm more interested in the now. I do have to mention I feel lighter, content and more present, which is a good thing.

WHAT IS GOING ON?

I'm amused at how quickly I adapt to different healing methods. Even my analytical mind has quietened down as though I'm accepting change and new techniques with ease and comfort. The healing team I work with are exceptionally talented, knowledgeable, loving and kind. It's as though they know my every thought, thirst, and capacity to receive new healing methods and techniques.

The healing I am being taught, shown and playing a part in, I could never have imagined. Yet somewhere along the journey, I have become calm and accepting. Even writing these words makes me laugh as I'm not naturally this way. Once a child scared of the dark, feared the spirit world and now, I have become hungry to absorb and learn as much as I can. The aim? To make a difference and properly help heal others.

I'm not playing at this. I'm on a mission to complete my chosen journey in the hope I won't have to come down here again and relearn what I was too scared of getting involved in. No, thank you! I've also become very aware of the passing of time and how precious it is. Life passes so quickly and should never be taken for granted.

I will not spend any more of my time worrying about what others think, as ultimately humans, if we are being honest, can be rather selfish, self-consumed and don't care what others are doing. Most decent people are not bothered, becoming more open-minded and accepting, as long as it doesn't hurt another.

So, what is it I'm reluctant to share? A strange occurrence happened whilst doing healing. Whilst healing a person, a different technique is being used. As I'm drawn to look in a certain part of the person's body, a red laser beam is being used to burn the outside of the shadow/stagnated energies with such precision, so it doesn't affect the surrounding tissues or hinders healing recovery time.

My eyes are directed to the outside of the dark shadow substance as though my eyes or third eye are controlling the procedure. I'm not consciously thinking about the procedure, it is just occurring naturally. Once again, as though I've done all of this before. Most things in life I have to work hard at to achieve good results, but this feels natural and with a sense of ease.

The atmosphere is intense, serious and disciplined with no room for error but perfectly natural. I know perhaps in another space or time, I have done this all before. I don't question, I simply do. I only start to relax when the removal of unwanted energy has successfully been removed, the space filled in with protection, cleansed, calmed down and healed.

You don't fully relax until you have been told the procedure is complete and start to come out of the light trance. My spirit healing team are the main healers who all have special healing gifts. I am simply part of the team, the channel or vessel used to pass onto the person. My job is to remove any form of myself or ego and let the healing take place.

I feel privileged to be chosen to be part of such a special team and even more honoured to be allowed to see what is happening. Why would they allow me to see? So, I could write about it to perhaps reassure others that work in the same way, that all of this is very real. And not to allow the self-doubting chitter chatter inside their heads to disrupt their journey. (That's my educated guess anyway, or at least, now you know, you are certainly not alone.)

A true healer should be able to put you straight at ease with their warmth and kindness. If you don't feel this and the person is self-consumed about perhaps all their qualifications, run a mile. For this person I would suspect hasn't removed their ego and hasn't been chosen to be part of a team to help others.

Word of mouth is usually the best; your gut

instinct is better. Sorry, I deviated but it really is important for the individual to choose wisely as there is good and bad in every walk of life. It's pitch black, early hours of the morning and I'm startled to an unusual sensation, as though there is a gently vibrating warmth roaming throughout my body. I go back into a light sleep but very aware I'm dipping deeper in and out of a meditative/trance state.

I'm very relaxed and accepting as I watch a red laser beam working methodically throughout my body's muscle fibres. I can see the laser beam melting down the intricate damaged tissue and the old scar tissue. The muscle fibres after being lasered look correctly aligned, pink and healthy. No longer like tough, ropey, zigzag knotted lumps of damaged tissue. The whole thing is fascinating as I've always had a deep interest in anatomy and physiology.

As I'm going in and out of a meditative state, I'm fully aware more is going on, but I'm not allowed access to every specific detail. Why is this? I don't know, perhaps this is a good thing. Before this incident occurred, I had noticed my energy had dropped significantly. I'm starting to notice a pattern that when I'm about to receive extreme healing, my energy is depleted to the point I can only fully physically and mentally relax and comply.

I lose any anxious feelings or worries of what could happen because I'm too calm and exhausted to care. This sensation always takes place just before an unusual or new healing approach to working on my physical and spiritual bodies happens. Once petrified, now I've learnt the art of stepping out of the situation and watching from a distance like an observer.

Nothing frightens me anymore, just a thirst to understand and an inner eagerness to get over the finish line. I'm so ready for all of this to be completed for it has been such a long journey. I am strong and won't be beaten by these unusual occurrences (That's an understatement!) but I am tired.

The next few days after the red laser treatment, I'm struggling to focus visually as my balance feels off. The fatigue is brutal. Yet I feel eerily calm. A calmness that almost doesn't feel part of me as though it belongs to another. The calmness is so intense it is verging on, strange choice of words, giving up!

Giving up caring about the outcome, no concern for what will happen next. It's like the fight has literally been sucked out of me, my spark is struggling to remain lit. I don't like this feeling, yet if I'm being totally honest, I'm too tired to care.

HERE WE GO AGAIN

I have these constant nagging words in my head. Why are you not spending time on healing yourself? You have the capability, so why are you not making time? These words are from my very direct, no-nonsense, very kind and lovely friend, Clarissa. She has been there throughout my journey and doesn't hold back on her advice, which I am eternally grateful for. "You have been told by spirit only you and them together can sort this out."

"So why aren't you?" Clarissa asked. Well, I can't really argue with that because she is right. Maybe I still don't fully believe I have the capability or perhaps I'm secretly hoping I can find a talented healer to take this all away. Still hoping for a miracle, I suppose. Nag, nag, nag, I keep hearing those words, "Jane, spend time healing yourself."

I'm so tired I can't be bothered. I know once I step into the healing dimension to help others, all fatigue disappears, so why am I so reluctant to spend time on myself? Fear of perhaps what I will uncover, I genuinely don't know. I make a conscious decision; I know there will be no one in the house for most of the day, so I need to discipline myself.

Don't get me wrong, I dedicate time to myself every day to meditate and receive healing with my spirit guides, but I don't lead. The house is empty, quiet and I've removed all distractions. I cleanse the space before bathing in the silence and eventually, I can feel myself drifting off into a blissful trance of nothingness. I send out my intention, where I am going, and exactly who I am with.

My intention is to journey to the upper world to connect to my sacred and divine healers to be shown how to heal myself with their help, now! When working in other dimensions, you must be direct, this initially might feel a little rude and abrupt, but you can't afford to get this wrong. You do not want to invite the wrong energy in. An example of this would be, to invite the most powerful energy in. Think about what you have just said.

The most powerful thing, is that the most powerful sacred and divine energy or could you have just invited in the most powerful dark energy in. Quite frightening that some healers are not using the right vocabulary. Your intention might be good and loving but your requests could be dangerous. That's why I'm not a fan of certain healing techniques you can obtain after a couple of days in a workshop.

With certain healing methods which shall not be

named, there is always an exchange of energy. The problem with this is, if the healer, for example, is vulnerable or has a weaker energy than the patient, the patient or animal will give their energy away to the healer. I have studied a variety of healing methods and they all have pros and cons, but in the wrong hands, without a shadow of doubt, could and can be disastrous.

So, to all those healers out there, whatever method you use, at least always stipulate that you want to connect to the sacred and divine energy, then you will at least be working in safety. This advice is coming from a good place, not to be an egotistical maniac, but to protect you and whoever you choose to work with. Sorry, I deviated.

Precise commands are vital and make it easier for the spiritual healers/beings to help us and ultimately, that is exactly what they want. Healing beings want to help us, it is us that puts all the barriers and complications in the way, never them. After sending out my intention, I'm immediately in the dimension I work in to heal others. I have become so accustomed to working in this dimension it only takes seconds to access.

I'm standing there staring into the strong, powerful yet gentle brown eyes of my Indian guide. I'm always met initially by him, as they know it brings me comfort, reassurance and puts me at ease. No words are spoken, we communicate through telepathy. A similar method whilst working as a medium, but more direct. It fascinates me how much more natural this feels than speaking in the material world.

I suppose this is because you don't have to filter or hide your true meaning. It is simple, as it is the truth. I'm directed by my spirit team to look at myself as I would a patient. I visualise the person in the healing dimension, but this time as a mirror image of me, as though a clone of myself stood in front of me. At first, I found it difficult to detach as I'm struggling with the image of myself.

Discipline kicks in as I treat the image as a person who needs healing and not emotionally related to me. I'm being shown that now I am detached from my physical self. I need to work on my physical and spiritual energy layers. Basically, in simple terms, I am in the healing dimension looking at a mirror image of myself which I need to heal. Blimey, I hope I didn't confuse you too much as I've struggled to write this.

I'm finding this a bit challenging as it feels unnatural. As I think these thoughts, I'm told firmly to concentrate. Which means remove yourself Jane, out of the situation and blend into the energy. Back into a light trance where I will be gently directed and taught what I need to do.

As I'm staring deep into my opposite self, I feel another healer's presence.

Medicine man approaches close into my energy field as I feel him swaying and moving around me. My eyes are instantly drawn to the left side of my body where I sense darkness and can see some sort of creature. I'm shown images of past fears and how I have allowed this creature to feed off me. I can see a mass of a thick black substance with what looks like human legs, but aren't formed properly and look misaligned and deformed.

The black creature/entity is wriggling and kicking out its legs as though refusing to be removed. It feels wedged deeply within my thoracic spine. Realising it has been spotted, it starts to burrow deeper into my chest cavity like a frightened large black beetle trying to hide. The creature appears to be succeeding. Medicine man expands larger as his energy becomes stronger and more powerful.

The strength and power of Medicine man's energy makes me feel fearless, unstoppable and mighty. This creature has no option other than to leave, now! The dark entity has been dislodged; it feels like it is screeching, a horrendous high pitch cry, yet I can't hear it. The vibrations of the high pitch screeching entity/thing is creating a strange vibrating and pulsing throughout my body, instantly making me shudder.

As the wriggling, screeching creature is removed from my chest cavity, two very tall dark beings appear from nowhere. These tall dark beings are silent, wearing dark black gowns with no detail on them. They have some form of headdress which makes them look like tall hats, but I know they are not. I am not able or given permission to see their faces. Where these tall, dark beings' faces should be, there is simply darkness, nothing.

I have seen these beings before but very rarely. The whole sensation goes from a battlefield trying to remove the entity to calmness, a nothingness. Like time has frozen still, deadly silent with a nothingness. The two tall dark beings take the entity/creature with them and vanish. I'm told the entity did not belong here and will be taken to the correct time, space, zone where it belongs and was only able to be removed because I had given permission.

The energy shifts back to working healing mode. The healing is not over, yet I can feel a sense of urgency to progress. I'm taken directly to the back of my neck. As I look closer, I can see a thick ropey cord coming directly out of the back of my head. I'm told this cord needs removing, for it has been draining me of all my energy. I see my

Indian guide's hands placed gently over my right hand as I'm guided with gentle precision and taught how to remove it.

The movement must be gentle so as not to cause shock or further damage. With a gentle twist and pull movement, the cord is removed. My other hand is guided to close the hole, whilst another guide steps in with a funnel of a swirly air substance, to remove the cord to once again where it should be. Not in the back of my head. As soon as I've witnessed the cord disappear out of sight, we work on filling in the hole with a grey clay substance so no more energy can leak out.

Another two healing beings step close in. The first to push in gold light and the second to place a blue substance over the area to calm and aid the healing process. Just as I think we have finished, I'm taken directly to my thoracic spine, upper back. I've always suffered extreme pain and discomfort from this area for as long as I can remember. As I'm shown my back, I can see several holes on either side of my spine. These holes are shaped in the formation of what you would imagine a pair of wings. (My instant thought, a fallen angel in a past life.)

The energy is seeping out and unprotected. The wings have been savagely removed exposing what look like deep, empty holes of eternity. I look inside and see what I would imagine space to look like. Pure pitch black with sparks of light resembling stars or planets. Gaping holes that go further in time, space, and eternity. I'm shocked to see what I have witnessed and for a split second I can feel myself coming out of the energy.

I remove all thoughts and submerge myself back into the healing. The healing feels serious as though we are working in a surgery repairing a deeply wounded person. Every deep hole needs sealing and protecting. The damage from previous lives is barbaric, cruel and unimaginable to the human mind. A surgical procedure using what looks like a sterile, steel needle is methodically inserted into the surrounding tissues to sew up the vast, gaping holes.

The surgery is led by another of my healing beings who is using advanced futuristic techniques. Futuristic means for those like me who didn't know, relating to or describing events in an imagined future. The problem with this word, for the human species to understand, is futuristic healing methods are just as real as this present moment, but more powerful.

The problem with what I have just said is scientists haven't got to the stage of proving it yet, but that doesn't mean it is unreal. Simply not discovered or perhaps hidden from humans?

Imagine if any of this was proven to be real in this time. What would the consequences be, especially perhaps financially? Thought-provoking, what does your gut instinct tell you, not your logical mind. I deviated again, but this time connecting to my spiritual guides and their input.

The healing procedure consists of a relay of my guides administering their different methods and techniques. Each healing being brings in their own unique gift. It's fascinating to have the privilege to watch and an honour to play a small part in it. Finally, the healing is complete. The energy becomes lighter as I'm put into a transparent cleansing funnel where I'm fully cleansed before fully relaxing.

I show my gratitude and respect before returning to the here and now. My mind is overactive as I replay repeatedly, what has just happened. I'm struggling to process what I have witnessed, even for me, that was a little too far. As I contemplate the realisation of what took place, I suddenly think of Eddie.

Eddie was a fantastic, no-nonsense medium and a trusted friend who I always turned to for advice when the mediumship became uncomfortably extreme. Sadly, he is no longer with us. I wish I could still speak to him in this world, it's all very nice sending thoughts to loved ones, but the presence and the sound of Eddie's voice always brought me comfort, reassurance and a loving calmness. I know he would have confirmed all of this to be true and then told me to pull myself together and just get on with it.

I smile and feel emotional as I imagine his rough cockney accent repeating the words. "Jane, it is what it is, just get on with it!" The next few days after revisiting the healing on myself, I'm fully aware it is time to put it in a box and move on. It's like I have a spiritual library where I put all these occurrences safely away knowing they are kept safe until it's time to return home.

Back home, heaven, another dimension whatever the individual chooses to believe. For some, this will mean an eternal death of nothingness. Wouldn't that be less complicated, rather relaxing and strangely comforting? Certainly, less intriguing and interesting. The truth of the matter is, we will all have to wait and see. The physical shell of the body in time will die, this is fact, but the soul lives on as I have witnessed time and time again.

Freedom of choice, believe whatever makes you feel happy and brings you comfort. Don't allow others, learnt fears and beliefs sway your inner knowing, follow what is right for you. After that experience, I feel different. Something within me has changed. I'm certainly not cured of my ailments, but I feel more whole. I feel fully contained within my physical body.

Still not fully balanced for I'm aware my soul/spirit isn't fully aligned, but I'm whole. My energy has slightly improved, tired, but not fatigued. I'm probably not making sense as I can't express these feelings, but I do know the change that has taken place is significant. So significant I can never return to my old self.

TIME TO PUSH THE BOUNDARIES OF WHAT I'VE BEEN TAUGHT

Throughout my spiritual journey, I decided I would not read about other mediums or healer's journeys for I needed to witness and experience my own truth. I'm a little sceptical of others until I'm proven different. I think this is healthy for we all have our own minds, gut instincts, and should make our own decisions.

Just because someone tells me, for example, fairies are real, I won't mock, but I will sit on the fence with an open mind until I witness it for myself. I've met too many people who will believe everything the teacher tells them. Yet teachers and people who we perceive in power of authority, don't know everything and do make mistakes.

I sound like a rule breaker. I'm not, I just need to learn from experiences of life, not from textbooks that often haven't evolved. If someone is running a development circle for mediumship, I need to see if they can connect with the spiritual world and prove it. If someone says they are a healer, I need to feel their presence and energy.

More importantly, if someone says they are any form of lightworker, I need to feel their kind, nurturing and loving energy to be satisfied. There are so many talented and gifted psychic/medium and healers, but they are not always particularly nice people. Unfortunately, sometimes, not always, they can allow their egos to take over and forget their true purpose, which is simply to help others.

To be honest, I've been very fortunate and always been led to very gifted, lightworkers who have openly shared all their wealth of knowledge and expertise. I feel eternally grateful to all those I have met, especially in my younger days. Whilst spending time flicking through messages on social media, which I must admit, I very rarely do, unless I'm sent a message from a friend, I saw a medical intuitive healer advertising a course.

Usually, I wouldn't give it a second thought, but my throat started constricting, letting me know there was some substance to this lady. I choose to ignore it. As you might have gathered by now, I'm not always compliant, even in spirit. A couple of days later, it literally keeps popping up. I'm intrigued, so I have a look at her course, see the price and think, forget it! Another week passes, and I can't get this woman's course out of my head.

I ask my spirit guides if I really need to know what this lady is teaching and will it help what I already know. My throat immediately constricts, making it absolutely crystal clear this is part of my development. I decided to research the lady. She seems the real deal, but I'm not paying extortionate money on a course that I can't afford. Bingo, she has written some books.

It's like all the information is in the book, so I decide to study it for myself and find out what information spirit wants me to learn. I'm not a fan of reading, as I tend to become a little restless. As I think these thoughts, my throat constricts. I can feel the presence of one of my more serious, very disciplined guides step closer as if directing me to just get on with it.

I have a little chuckle to myself as all my guides who I work with are very strong, no-nonsense characters, which I must admit I prefer, as I don't think a delicate, overly gentle, nurturing soul would work for me. I correct myself; it could work, but would take a lot longer to achieve the same outcome and the angelic spirit, I'm sure would find me infuriating.

The spirit world is so clever they know exactly what spirit guides work best with certain people. Actually, I correct, myself again. I do have one gentle lady guide who works with me when channel writing and she is clear, precise, and wonderful to work with. Ultimately, I leave it to the spirit world, as they have higher intelligence in every aspect and know what works for us best. Thank goodness!

The book has arrived. I made a conscious decision, however bored I might feel reading it, I will read every page and complete the book. I'm a starter and a completer so there is no excuse not to finish and I'm on a mission to find out what it is I need to take from this book. As I look at the book, I am filled with dread as I really can't be bothered. As I'm thinking that my throat constricts implying, just get on with it.

Much to my surprise the book is quite interesting and what is more fascinating is this lady works in a similar way as I do. She explains in detail what she sees when working in the spirit realms, again very similar. Even the cleansing method the spirit world uses on her is almost the same as what I experience. Blimey, this woman works very similarly to me!

I'm intrigued to learn more about this lady as she too started off as a medium, although it was considered normal in her childhood and accepted. My childhood was completely different, no understanding of the communication of the spirit world, and no guidance. She had embraced her gifts and I had fought my gifts, fiercely all the way.

Other than that major difference, we spoke the same language. I found reading her book comforting as I hadn't met another, who worked using the same method. I've met loads of people who work as mediums and use gentle healing methods, but never anyone who even spoke of the advanced surgical techniques and looking inside people's physical bodies.

You could argue there might be a reason for not oversharing, I totally get why it is safer to stay silent! As I continue to read her book, I identify my own weaknesses, by listening to experienced others rather than being brave enough to do what felt natural, I'd got the balance wrong.

What do I mean? Protection, some teach it's all about your intention, so if you are working in a loving way, you will be protected. Wrong! I found that one out by myself. Others believe in rituals of protection, almost becoming obsessive over protection procedures. I have always suspected and felt this to be wrong as the person is putting too much emphasis on protecting themselves then surely an element of fear will creep in.

If you are always predicting danger or attack of darker energies, then you could attract it. So, the jury is out. This lady talked openly about using certain methods to expand your energy. Embrace your light. She talked freely about how spirits were just the same as us, but without bodies and meant us no harm and could do us no harm.

I liked the way she normalised mediumship and removed the fear aspect out of it. I brought into it for a while until I noticed, in my opinion, that there weren't many boundaries. In all walks of life, there must be balance. A time to work and a time to say no more. I was taught discipline from Eddie. When I first met Eddie, I hadn't learnt how to control my gifts and was visited by the spirit world relentlessly.

They weren't contacting me, to frighten or scare me, simply intrigued by my energy. They often wanted to gain access to their loved ones. It was a frightening and exhausting time. It took a lot of discipline, courage and bravery to take control. Thank goodness, I had Eddie to guide me, for it was bloody awful.

You can't help everyone, and certainly not at the expense of your health, physically and more importantly mentally. The first and most important thing Eddie taught me was when to allow spirit access to work with me and more important, the ability to say, "No, not now." I believe you need to be living functionally in this material world. You can't if you are constantly talking to spirit beings.

It would be exhausting and, in my opinion, wrong for we are on earth to experience and learn the same as everyone else. Now, I'm questioning her method. I appreciate her method might work successfully for some; however, we are all working at different levels. I made the decision that her method is not quite right for me, but I'm now fully aware I haven't fully got the balance right.

By being at times too overprotective of my energy, I haven't been allowing my energy to expand enough. Perhaps I've been a little too controlling of my mediumship and need to let go a little. Lightbulb moment! I start to reflect on myself and how I have perceived my journey. First thought, if I'm constantly overprotecting how is it perceived in the spirit world?

In the spirit world, would a dampened light constantly trying not to draw attention to itself be interpreted as a person scared, vulnerable and not fully in charge of her abilities? Secondly, why haven't I expanded my inner light fully, as I know how to. Surely the brighter I shine, the more I will attract attention from the spirit world. But it will also repulse the darker energies away. Ultimately, having a healthier balance with my gifts will naturally aid me.

I conclude that I need to wear my big girl pants and challenge this theory. It's time to expand my light/energy and find out for myself. There is an exercise in the book that uses a technique to expand your energy which in theory should increase your energy. I shall not divulge the technique as it could be disastrous, especially for less experienced people and I believe could frighten them.

I know from experience in my younger days, I wouldn't have known how to control this. A bit of fun for some, but not if the person has natural gifts that perhaps they might not be aware of. Once Pandora's box has been opened, there is no going back. Especially for people who have been chosen to work with spirit.

Before continuing, I check with my spirit team if there is any benefit to doing this exercise and if it will help my development as it goes against what I have learnt. My throat constricts, I'm given permission and strongly encouraged. Interesting, why? I spend dedicated time practising expanding my energy and sensing, feeling and absorbing the new energy I'm accessing.

After several weeks I can access this new method with ease and I've seen a slight improvement in my energy levels. I'm feeling stronger within myself and more confident. I've also noticed whilst healing others or accessing dimensions, I'm more confident, accepting and strong. It's like I'm starting to embrace who and what I am, without questioning everything.

Even after the most extreme session working with my healing guides to remove darkness out of another, I'm comfortable with it. I like this new method, for it enables me to understand I still have further to go to reach my full potential. You can't reach your full potential if you are not prepared to shine brighter. Protection is very important, but it must not be allowed to stifle your capabilities.

Fear can be powerful, but only if we allow it to grow in strength. I was once taught there is nothing to fear in life. Fear is manifested from within, and it doesn't need to exist if you take control. Blimey, how times have changed! I hear your thoughts, easier said than done. I totally agree, but we could all challenge it, even if just a little bit. I'm also encouraged by my spirit guides to spend more time getting to know as much as I can about my sacred and divine healing guides.

The more time I spend and blend in their energy, the stronger our healing to help others will become. It is important to know who you are working with on the other side for it naturally increases trust, a strong bond and in time, knowing you are in safe hands. Ultimately through time, you don't question your safety, for time and time again you are proven how loved, safe and protected you are.

Dedication, commitment, and most important

time. Without putting in the time, you can't fulfil your true potential. (Sorry too preachy, true though!) So, I found the bit I needed from the book. I discovered there are probably lots of people out there who work in a similar healing way. A topic that is not openly shared. Why? Could it offend others? Doesn't everything in life offend someone?

I love diverse, wacky and thought-provoking conversations for it makes me question things. I enjoy my thoughts and views being challenged and I must admit I've been proven several times to be wrong. I have learnt often there is so much not discussed due to fear of ridicule or being perceived as inappropriate. Freedom of speech, so valuable, but I'm not one hundred percent convinced there is such a thing anymore.

I deviated, whoops! The main thing I learnt from the book was that it is healthier for your body and welfare to expand your energy. Suppressing your natural gifts will result in never fully completing your earthly journey. Basically, be brave enough to be yourself! I disagreed with a lot of what I read, as she didn't promote protecting your energy.

I had been suppressing my light too much which I take full responsibility for, while she was teaching students to constantly shine bright. Great, but only if the student can control their energy. We have all met someone who zaps and drains the energy out of you with their negativity. In this instance, I would immediately put up an imaginary barrier directly in front of them, between the two of us.

I always imagine a large, thick, metal barrier. Like in an old-fashioned movie where the bank is being robbed, someone manages to hit the panic button and immediately the metal volt draws down. Sounds a little make-believe, but what you are doing is setting boundaries. Yes, you continue to be loving and supportive but you don't let the other person drain from your energy source.

With practice it becomes second nature, eventually you end up doing it automatically with shall we say, the less vibrant, lower energy, basically life energy zappers. They will still get your help, support and lending ear, but you won't feel dreadful and tired after being in their presence. I don't believe you should turn your back on these people, just be aware of how to protect your energy and maybe ration how much time you spend with them.

So, folks that's what I took from a book I was guided to read by spirit. I'll read another if I'm guided to, but as I have said from the start, I like to discover things by experiencing them and I'm usually guided away from reading other's stories. I need to stay true to myself and remain authentic.

THE PACE IS PICKING UP

Expanding my energy more frequently has given me a more carefree feeling towards my spiritual journey. It's like a light bulb moment; an awakening to how I'm supposed to be. Everything feels lighter, easier and natural. Removing the preconceived taught obstacles has allowed me a wonderful feeling of freedom. I feel quite emotional as I write these words for, I'm only just discovering how encaged I felt.

The spirit world only gives you access at the right time on your journey, therefore there is no point pushing forwards. You might think you are progressing forwards if you compare your connection to others, especially whilst demonstrating in psychic/mediumship. The reality is, we are not here to compare ourselves to others as we all have completely different paths. In my younger days I was so keen to prove the survival of death.

I pushed and pushed for more evidence in hope that one day, I would blow the minds of scientists. The harsh reality was a scientist would always question mediumship as their argument will always be, that there simply isn't enough evidence. Also, I wonder how it would affect religious beliefs. I suspect there would be a refusal of acceptance and denial. So, looking at my previous behaviour, it was a little naive.

I still hope one day, a medium will prove the scientist wrong and it will have to be fully accepted and even respected. So out of my own naivety, that's why I became ill. An obsession on proving and perfecting, rather than really listening to what and how spirit wanted me to work. I was very naive and foolish. They wanted me to write which isn't as exciting as connecting for a loved one in spirit and healing the heart of another.

Maybe it was the praise and appreciation from a fellow human I secretly craved. Finally, perhaps being acknowledged for being good at something. I do not doubt this. But by not listening and doing what I wanted instead of listening, I've had to go an extremely long way around to get to where I was supposed to be.

I can now honestly say, I still find writing a chore, especially writing my story, as it doesn't come naturally but perhaps in time it will help more people. (I have to mention I find channel writing an honour and pure joy, but that's because I'm channelling.) As for being allowed the honour of healing with my guides, I can't think of anything else that not only fascinates, fulfils and humbles me, but makes me feel blissfully happy, truly alive and whole.

The beauty of working at a higher level is it doesn't take any of your energy. In fact, it gives you energy and you receive healing. A beautiful exchange with spirit. I occasionally do mediumship, but only when given permission by my spiritual guides. It must be to help another; I'm certainly not going to use my energy or health to entertain another. That lesson has been learnt!

I had no intention of writing the above, but I know these words will resonate with so many of you who work as lightworkers and those who might in the future be led to work with spirit. Let your gifts unravel naturally. Remain open-minded to exploring different avenues if it feels right. If you have been chosen to work specifically for spirit, you will eventually work as they want.

Don't kid yourself, you have engineered your path for there really is a more beautiful, divine and sacred energy bigger and more powerful than us mere mortals. Thought-provoking, if nothing else! With opening and expanding my energy has become more responsibility. More responsibility to remain calm, objective and accepting. The ability to observe, step a little further out of the experience and remove human fear.

Somewhere along the way, I seem to be losing more and more fear which is wonderful. Fear is exhausting, not good for you physically or mentally. I'm so grateful to have been taught the ability to respect fear and my emotions, but not become consumed or controlled by it anymore. I know this has to happen to get to wherever I am being led. Fascinating, once you learn to step out of preconceived and often taught beliefs.

The fun begins. Tony has gone away due to work commitments. It's the early hours of the morning, pitch black. I've woken up startled as I feel I've lost something very important. As I come around, I start to rationalise to myself everything is fine, as I haven't lost anything. As I calm down and can feel myself start to drift off, my heart starts to flutter and I become anxious.

After a strong word with myself, my chest is still fluttering. I step out of the situation emotionally and look on with fascination rather than previously with fear. As I lie there awake, I purposely go into a meditative/trance state, as that's what I'm instructed to do. Here we go! My jaw is forced into precise end range positions as I can hear tiny muscle fibres being torn and realigned.

There is an excruciating piercing pain that feels like a razor-sharp object being plugged between a space in my left ribs.(Intercostal muscles). I take a deep breath and start to detach myself from my physical body and visualise myself looking down upon myself. The pain is unbearable. I feel lightheaded, nauseous, as though I'm going to pass out.

Fear is starting to creep back in as I refuse entry and rationalise there has been too much time invested in me for anything to go wrong. The pain starts to subside as I can feel muscle fibres within my chest cavity being gently moved, as though trying to get towards my shoulder blade.

I feel another sharp object like a surgical metal, long needle, or probe being plunged directly through my left nipple, again between the ribs. I can feel the object moving around trying to find access to the back of my shoulder blade. It's like I have something hidden behind my left scapular that needs removing, what is it? I don't know.

The pain is becoming heightened as I'm frantically trying to use all my trance methods to escape the agony. As I submerge myself into a meditation/trance state, I look on with fascination and intrigued at the precision of such intricate movements. Just as I think I'm managing the pain, my shoulders are elevated, lifting my head up, forced to the side in an end range position.

The jaw starts to move repeatedly, opening and closing the mouth, with the tongue moving rapidly in strange circular and erratic motion. I can hear the jaw clunking and making horrific crunching and grinding noises. I need this to end. The razor-sharp probe inserted through my chest cavity, directly through my left nipple feels like it is plunging through my heart. I can't take it anymore. I've lost all ability to stay in a calm meditative/trance state.

The movements throughout my body have taken over. I can't bear the pain, yet I'm too frightened to intervene with the process, for I could do more damage than good. It continues, the extreme pain. My jaw moving, my body shaking and being moved as though completely taken over by a higher, more intelligent source. I feel so sick with the pain, I feel myself slipping into trance, but this time as though I'm going to faint.

Nothing! Silence! A calmness within the room that feels eerie. I'm lying there pale, clammy and shaken. I'm shown an image of a blue substance being injected into the area of the underside of my left scapular, seeping into the chest cavity.

Amused by the image but I know not to question it and realise I'm another step closer to the finish line. I plead with them to finish this process, but I also know there is nothing either of us on our different sides of the veil can do to quicken the final outcome.

I'M BECOMING BRAVER

I feel awful. My balance has regressed. I'm back on a boat in the depths of a storm at sea. I feel nauseous. I can feel my spirit swirling within my body, fighting to find the right connection, to feel fully settled and balanced. I won't lie, I'm dwelling a little in self-pity for I can't do anything to ease the swaying within my body. A bit dramatic, but sometimes I feel like a caged bird trying to find freedom from this damn shell that keeps me alive.

Alive, I don't feel fully alive, but trapped. Perhaps some might think I'm being ungrateful. Yes, I agree. But that is how I feel when I'm having a bad spell. Well on a positive note, it reminds me to remember to appreciate and value how I felt before. I never allow myself to succumb to self-pity for long, as I'm fully aware of the depths of darkness and self-sabotage.

In the past it has dragged me down and pulled me under, submerged in the depths of cold, murky, dark water almost losing the ability to see the light, let alone the ability to breathe. Right moan over, move on Jane! I remind myself this will pass for nothing can stay the same forever. I am strong, I am healthy, I am full of energy, and I am perfectly balanced. I must stay focused on telling my physical body how to feel and behave.

The body will only believe what you tell it as truth and fact. The body only knows what we say as truth. Why would we lie to ourselves? The problem with this is the body hears our deepest thoughts and then creates physiological changes, so we must push through feelings of hopelessness and trust in our body's healing capability and how powerful we are. How we talk to ourselves is vital.

If you constantly tell yourself you can't achieve or get better, the odds are stacked against you. I challenge you to notice how you speak to yourself, your daily thoughts, it's a real eye-opener. Most of us aren't aware how harsh we are on ourselves. If you find this is the case, challenge yourself to changing your self-talk to a more loving and self-accepting approach. It really is difficult, but gradually becomes a little easier.

There has been a lot of research proving time and time again just how powerful our thoughts are. I try to remain disciplined with positive self-talk and trusting in the process. There is no flowering it up, it is hard, a daily challenge. It helps having a strong connection with my spiritual guides who have assured me I have already succeeded.

As I have mentioned before, I have been shown a glimpse into my future, and I would have to be fully recovered. I don't doubt my future. I was visited in the early hours of the morning by Eddie. A talented healer, medium, and more importantly, a friend who had passed over several years ago. He came back to tell me, this journey on earth is an illusion, one we create by ourselves, so therefore there doesn't need to be as much suffering.

He wished he had known that when he was alive, for he really didn't need to suffer. Is there any substance or truth to Eddie's words? The truthful answer is I don't know, yet I do know Eddie only ever spoke the truth. My gut instinct, although it perhaps feels ridiculous to the logical mind, feels correct. I just haven't fully worked out how to overcome the suffering of this world.

After a couple of days, usually the swaying sensation and nausea subsides. I then have a strict word with myself to be grateful for the health I have. Much to my horror, I feel like I'm regressing. Unfortunately I know there is absolutely nothing I can do, other than, to sit quietly through the storm, stay calm and trust it will settle. Still no improvement, what the heck!

I come to my own conclusion, I feel so ill, I at least need to do something to help myself. It's a gamble as I know if you try to push through things spiritually and your body is not ready to adjust, you can make things a lot worse. Decision made, I'm going into the upper spiritual realms and find out whether I can help myself or even if I'm given permission to.

As I lie on my bed in the silence and darkness of my room, I send out my intentions. My intention is to connect to my sacred and divine healing partners to be healed, now! As I fully relax and submerge myself into a light trance, I'm greeted by my Indian guide, which fills my heart with a blissful sensation of familiar love, comfort and strong protection. I ask what it is that is causing this extreme fatigue and unbalance rocking sensation.

I'm shown crystal clear the devil card from the tarot pack. The devil card resembles, for me, self-sabotage. I'm made aware I'm sabotaging my own energy with self-doubt and an inability to fully believe in my own power and strength. It's partly me creating the lack of equilibrium within my shell due to not accepting my true purpose. Not what I wanted to hear, but brutally honest!

Through a form of telepathy from my guide, I'm told exactly what to send out for help. As my Indian guide relays the thoughts I'm saying with authority and precision to the gatekeeper to allow a sacred and divine specialist to remove all cords, entities, spirits and energies,

I have created or allowed access to me in past lifetimes and including up to the present. Now! I lie in silence, no thoughts, just bathing in nothingness.

I feel myself dropping into a slightly deeper meditative/trance state. I don't expect anything and know I will only receive what is best for me. Bathing in nothingness and a beautiful inner peace. My heart fills with joy as though singing. Out of nowhere, the energy changes from a calmness to an almost frantic rushing business. I can see a strange, funny and very short looking man rushing around me as though we are already running out of time.

He has a black rucksack on his back, but it is in the shape of a rectangular box. I can see he is holding onto a device which literally looks like a long tube of a hoover. I start to question the reality of what I'm seeing as he looks like a character, for those of you old enough to remember, ghostbusters. You couldn't make this up, and I haven't got the creativity or imagination, or the desire to come up with this.

I'm so amused by the presence of this being. I can feel myself coming out of trance and weakening the connection. I hear the word firmly, "Discipline!" from my Indian guide. I'm fully submerged in the moment. I watch this short, jolly character work around my body. He is precise and very quick as though hoovering up all energy that no longer serves me. He spends longer on the left side of my body, the chest, eye and lower back.

Cords and shadow formations are fully removed internally and externally from my physical and spiritual layers. Layers upon layers that I wasn't fully aware we consisted of. I try to take a closer look at his face which he is immediately aware of and comes up directly into my face. He has good humour and I sense him laughing. "You weren't expecting a normal looking bloke to be given this job, were you?"

We aren't all angelic looking; you earn your job in these realms, there is no discrimination of those without wings." He said as he was laughing hard and loud. His energy feels pure, loving and earthy. What do I mean by earthy? A grounded being that hasn't forgotten the human aspect of the soul and is relatable. He has warmth, likeability and is comforting to be around.

When I meet a different spiritual being I'm always a little suspicious initially until I thoroughly check them out. I have an analytical mind and don't believe in just what I see. I need to sense, see and know what I think before asking my guides for confirmation. The higher level you work within the spiritual realms, I've noticed the more you are protected.

If the spirit world has chosen you specially to help others, they will have invested a lot of time in you, generally from birth. Your protection increases as you work in more extreme situations. Thank goodness! I don't take any of this for granted and feel it is important not to become complacent. To continue to check all other energies is a must and can only develop and enhance your gifts.

Trust is vital, I totally agree, but not checking for yourself is taking a risk. Some will disagree with this, fine, we all have different opinions. I deviated! I can feel and sense the energy around my body changing as though this cheerful man has almost completed the removal of all past and present energies that don't belong to my body. As I look at my body, I'm shown lots of individual gold rings as though encasing each vertebrae of the spine.

The gold rings start at the bottom of my spine running the length of the spine to the final vertebrae at the base of my skull. I watch as I can see my spine being gentle and strategically moved. I'm mesmerised by the subtle swaying and the beauty of the golden rings. As I'm staring, transfixed on what is occurring, I see out of the corner of my eye an exceptionally tall dark being.

I have seen these beings throughout my journey.

The being brings a sense of command, authority and power. There are no sensations of fear, danger or darkness around it, yet there isn't pure love and light around it. The being feels of nothingness. I have come up with my own conclusion on this being, it is a perfect species of both. A being of perfect equilibrium, yin and yang, light and dark.

A species that consists of pure love, goodness, angelic, and yet darkness, and dare I say, evil. This being always baffles me as I should feel afraid, yet I feel at peace, calm and an eerie nothingness. I have asked my guides about this being and they have confirmed I am correct, however not to overanalyse. I always feel a heightened sense of protection around me when these beings appear as well as the nothingness.

I haven't quite got my head around these beings, but I know their purpose will become more apparent as my journey unravels. I have a confession to make, I also now know they have been with me throughout this lifetime from birth, but only appeared to me when I was mature enough to cope with the concept. I need to understand more. I feel no fear in the nothingness energy, so I directly ask the tall dark being if it is sacred and divine.

The reply I receive is, "I am pure, sacred and divine and also, dark and evil when required." I feel absolutely no horror to these words, just a thirst to understand. "What do you mean?" I ask. "We work to serve the lighter beings and walk as you humans think amongst the angels. We have two sides like humans, good and bad, light and dark. Most living species can't live or survive without both.

We serve chosen lightworkers to enhance their healing gifts, so they have the capability to remove darkness from others. A true healer must often heal, by having the capability to remove darkness, attachments and entities from another. A selfless and dangerous act if not fully protected. Healing cannot take place without the removal first of darkness. The dark elements are often self-created due to fear, self-loathing and trauma.

Unfortunately, this also occurs by attachments, entities and evil from other humans. Healers strive to work in love and light which is honourable but must accept whether they chose to believe, darkness is always present. Those who are chosen will be given the ability and protection to work with darkness. Removing darkness! There is light and dark in everything, especially in healing.

You have chosen and accepted to work healing and helping those with darkness attached to them. This is selfless, you have such a desire to help others, you are willing to risk your own safety. This is why you are now ready to progress forward. You have a choice to make, to move forward and receive full protection, you must give us permission to surround you fully.

Jane, if you decide to go ahead, your life will never be the same again. All your fears, self-sabotaging and sorrows will be moved into the light. You will not be the same person Jane, for the past will no longer exist. We will surround and protect you, but not be within you. The decision you make is for eternity." Blimey, not too big a decision to make then! Fear sets in, my mind has too many questions, I'm losing the connection.

I pull myself together, calm down, and submerge myself back into the trance state. I tell them I need more time and I'm not willing to rush into this decision which is received with acceptance. As I come out of the energy, I can feel myself asking a hundred questions. Eternity! I really need to get this one right.

I'M SAT STUCK ON THE FENCE

I could really do with someone to talk to about this situation. I'm thinking of Clarissa, but I think this could frighten her as I know all of this isn't her cup of tea. I decide to leave it for a few days to process before speaking first to spirit directly, then maybe Clarissa. It's first thing in the morning and whilst I'm doing my morning Qi Gong (like Tai Chi, basically gentle movements incorporating breath work), I can feel myself drifting off, daydreaming.

I'm overcome with the strange sensation/energy of nothingness, as I can see out of the corner of my eye a tall, dark being. As I continue the Qi Gong, I'm fully aware of the presence and feel almost comforted by its protective energy. Whilst exercising, I notice the being has placed his hand on my right shoulder. I should be freaking out, but I'm consumed by the sensation and calmness of nothingness.

As I look at the enormous lengthy thin hand, I notice how narrow, long, thin and malnourished the fingers are. I can only see three fingers which are covered in a thin, grey, almost transparent covering. The hand I imagine to be human, yet it is not. The first thought I have is, it is how you would imagine, the hand of death! A tall dark being wearing a dark cloak resembling death.

My gut instinct tells me this is incorrect, but I can't work out what this being looks like. When and if the time is ever right, I will be shown, but for now seeing the hand is enough. As I continue with the Qi Gong movements, I can physically feel the pressure of this hand upon my right shoulder and yet still I'm not perturbed. The hand is neither warm or cold, it is a perfect balance of both, a nothingness.

I can now see several other tall dark beings surrounding me in a circle formation. The number of these beings is increasing rapidly; it's as though they are a separate species from another dimension. As they approach nearer into my space, I see they are blending and integrating with what appears to be hundreds of light beings, sacred, divine lightworkers. The mixture of energies/beings seem to be happy and working in unison with one another. Why? I don't know yet!

As I'm watching with fascination, I'm being taught and shown how these tall dark beings walk freely amongst, some would say the angelic realms. It's as though these tall dark beings are protectors of the higher realms. I'm then told I can't fully heal or heal others without the desire and ability to remove the darkness. These tall, dark beings are here to teach me how to remove the darkness within me first and then others.

As desperate as I am to make a full recovery, I need more time to sense, feel and know what is right for me. I won't sell my soul, not even for health. I also know this is not the case, but I need to feel happy and take full responsibility for my decision. I need more time to process and speak to my guides. My decision is respected as they know as well as I know this story has already been written.

As I come out of the energy, I should be frantically overanalysing, yet I'm not. I ask myself, "Does any of this feel evil and dark?" The answer is no! It feels balanced and truthful. Don't get me wrong, I would rather be shown love, light and perfection in the realms but then, would I?

No, I want to be shown the truth, all sides, however challenging. I need to know what I'm getting into, especially if it will benefit others and myself. How times have changed. When and how did I become courageous? Nothing in life is given to us that we can't handle, although at times, we all feel vulnerable.

SO, WHAT SHOULD I DO?

I decided to write down all my concerns and ask my spirit guides for guidance and truth. My main concern is what do they mean when these tall dark beings will surround me. I'm told quite frankly, exactly that. My guides explain in simple terms I am not fully protected to help heal others without it potentially affecting my health. To fully heal others, you must have the ability to often remove darkness before true healing can take place.

If I choose to accept the protection of these beings, no harm can come near me. Including spirit energies that can gain access to mediums, without first being fully checked and given permission. No harm will be allowed anywhere near me. I will always be fully protected. Eternity seems a little extreme, really, forever I asked? "Forever, Jane!" Nothing like breaking the truth gently, I think to myself. Now for my main concern.

These beings will surround me, protect me, but I need to make sure they are fully aware as they have already mentioned they don't come directly into my physical body. "That is correct Jane. They will surround and protect you only. You will be able to feel, sense and at times see them, but they will not work within you." said my spirit guides. I then proceeded to ask the last question several more times.

It made sense to be protected, for my healing was becoming stronger and more extreme, but I needed to know I would remain myself. A pure channel, without the interference of a much stronger energy/being, I didn't fully understand, being given full access to me! Okay, starting to make logical sense, for I knew I couldn't continue to work the way I was without health repercussions and to be honest without full protection, it was dangerous.

The way I saw it, I needed to take the protection, or walk away from working with spirit completely. The latter, I had tried years ago, but my gifts only became stronger. Eddie said to me years ago after a closed circle session, in his rough cockney accent, "Jane, most mediums get to choose if they want to work with spirit, you, my love, have no choice. So, I suggest you just get on with it!"

I'm laughing as I can remember his voice and the way he always spoke so directly. You were never given what perhaps you wanted to hear, but you were always told the truth. I know exactly what he would tell me to do, but this was my choice.

CONFIRMATION

A few days pass and I have made my mind up, I know what I need to do. I've made my decision, but I'm intrigued to hear my valued and trusted friend Clarissa's opinion. I explain to her about the tall dark beings which I have now named Equilibrium beings. Equilibrium means a state in which opposing forces are balanced. These beings are half light and half dark, a perfect balance of both.

You can't fully say they are pure or evil for they are, I suppose, a perfect species of both. Get your head around that! I won't lie, it has taken me a lot of soul-searching to accept their presence. Before I begin, I ask Clarissa to try and remove all fear and concerns and just listen. As she listens intently, I can feel she is uncomfortable with what I'm telling her.

I explain in detail that the Equilibrium beings will need to blend with my energy initially to remove all traces of fear and energy that no longer serves me, to fully progress forwards. I reiterate several times that they will not be within me, but by my side for protection. This will ensure no other energy can harm me, which will enable me to heal at a higher level.

To have the ability and strength to heal others, all fear must be eliminated. I can't be fully protected without them. I start to giggle nervously as I say, "Oh yes, I forgot to mention if I accept, this is for eternity!" Clarissa remains in silence, deep in thought, before she admits she is not comfortable with any of what I have told her.

She tells me she doesn't like the sound of working with any form of darkness, even if it is just half of these Equilibrium beings. Silence again, I know Clarissa is asking her guides for clarity. "I can't believe I'm going to say this, but it feels the right thing to do. Spirit has never let you down, Jane. They know what they are doing, so you've got to get on with it."

"You are already in far too deep, so you have got to go for it! As you have said, you can't work at this level unprotected, for it's not safe. It's like they are testing your commitment to spirit. You must jump through these hoops. It feels the right thing to do. Let them blend with you in the way they need to enhance and protect you," said Clarissa. I had already made my decision, but needed to talk it aloud, with someone I could trust. I then explained to Clarissa, I had witnessed so much throughout some of the healings I had done.

Not all, but a significant amount of helping to heal others was reconnecting the person with a lost soul part which usually occurred when they were a child. Once you have experience meeting and reconnecting a child with their grown-up self, it can be a little overwhelming. I couldn't leave a frightened children in constant perpetual fear, stranded in other dimensions, when I could do something to help, for that would be morally wrong.

Clarissa said, "That is why they have chosen you; you are maternal and wouldn't let a child suffer. So, you are pretty, stuffed really, so just get on with it!" We both burst out laughing before I said, "Yep, that's about right, pretty stuffed!" Clarissa then went on to say that I needed to keep her updated on how I got on.

I expressed my concerns that I hoped whatever took place didn't affect my health and that I was ready to commit tomorrow. I burst out laughing before I said, "Bloody hell, Clarissa, I didn't see this one coming and I've still got to get these books finished. What will be will be, I'm not going to worry about the outcome as I know as strange as it sounds, this story has already been written."

GOING INTO THE UNKNOWN

What was it I said? Something about not worrying. I think I might have been exaggerating the truth and having a courageous moment. I'm feeling a little apprehensive, for I know what I'm about to do is for eternity. Oh well, here goes! I send my intention to the upper world to connect to my sacred and divine healers to receive the next part of my journey.

Within a second, I stood face to face and stared into the very serious, deep brown eyes of my Indian guide. His presence always brings me inner peace and reassurance, but the energy feels different. The intensity of the energy is very significant and formal. A white cloak is draped over my shoulders. As I look down, I discover I'm wearing a white garment, best described as an old fashioned, white long-sleeved nightie.

My Indian guide steps forward with great intensity, staring straight into eyes before saying, "Jane, do you accept the protection of the higher beings, this will be for eternity?" He repeats the sentence another two times. I want to say yes, but I'm a little hesitant. I already knew they surrounded me and when I look back on my journey, they have always been there, but I hadn't been given full access to their true form and capabilities.

A wave of courage and clarity fills my body with an inner knowing and wisdom I didn't know I possessed. I have no doubt that my next step forward is of great importance, loving and pure. With a clear intention, and no doubt in my mind, I said, "Yes, I accept and for eternity." I immediately saw two beings standing on either side of me. I can't see their faces, but they look like they are dressed in some sort of metal armour completely covering their bodies.

As soon as I get a glimpse, they vanish. I can feel their presence, but I'm not permitted to see them. The protection of these beings feels strong, fierce and shielding. I feel overcome with a heightened sensation of superior warrior courage, as though I'm fully aware no one or thing can come near me. As I'm bathing in this fearless extreme energy I'm distracted by the sight of my healing guides surrounding me in a circular formation.

I can see several other light beings surrounding them. I can't see them individually, but I can see the light of their presence. I can see the tall dark Equilibriums surrounding within and around the circle. I won't lie, I'm relieved to see the Equilibrium beings are keeping a respectful distance. They stand just outside my main healers, but amongst the other light beings.

I notice there is an utmost respect for the Equilibriums, as though they are from a higher dimension/realm who knows, but they are highly respected. I'm made fully aware there will be no other, lower energies including humans allowed access to my energy. I am now fully protected. Knowing this brings me comfort, reassurance and I can feel myself relax, sigh, and fully breathe.

I feel stronger, self-assured with the power/gifts I have been given to fully use them. No more doubting thoughts. I feel focused, fearless and a lighter sensation of freedom within my heart as though a weight has been lifted. For a few seconds, I feel a pure white energy as though it has exploded within what feels like my spirit/soul. A sense of heightened euphoria fills every cell, organ, muscle fibre, my whole body of love, happiness, peace and finally inner calmness.

My Indian guide steps forward and I'm told to relax for the healing process will be rapid. I'm instructed to continue making time daily for them to access my energy in private. I can feel myself drifting off into a light trance, completely free of previous self-created barriers. I feel like weeping for the sense of freedom is beautiful. I was never aware of how imprisoned I truly was until I became free.

Here we go, my jaw starts to open wide as my shoulders are slightly elevated and my head is flicked back repetitively towards my upper spine. The surrounding muscles are being released as warm fluid within my head is being moved. My head is violently shaken and moving so rapidly from side to side, it would literally look to others as though I had been possessed and out of a frightening horror movie.

With my new sense of freedom, I calmly continue to trust the process. My facial muscles are now being worked on as I can feel the deep facial muscle fibres being twisted and distorted into unusual positions. I can hear a subtle tearing sound taking place in my face. I'm physically tired, as I'm disciplining myself to remain relaxed and in trance.

I can feel my eyes aching and the fatigue setting in as my physical body struggles to keep up with the power of the spirit world. I have pain in my forehead and sinus area from all the intensity and extreme healing. I'm struggling to hold myself in the trance as all of a sudden, my chin is forced to my chest and I'm sat up. I can see and feel the hands of an Equilibrium being placed on my shoulders. I feel a powerful sense of nothingness!

Silence, as though time has stood still. I can see the lower part of my body is not connected fully to the rest of my body. There is a line of what looks like a beam/light of fire running across my lower pelvis. I can see the body gently swaying as though struggling to remain together. As I watch on, the Equilibrium is carefully realigning my body with such precision, delicacy and mastery.

Finally, my lower body is fully connected, the swaying stops, as I'm balanced and whole. As the Equilibrium steps back, my healers take over. The fun begins, the upper body, neck and head are thrown around aggressively as though forcing the body to fully connect, including the spinal fluids. Finally, it stops.

Silence and a sense of calmness and order returns. I thank my healing guides and the Equilibrium protectors, cleanse and disconnect before returning fully to the material world. I must explain each time I work within the higher realms I always go through a full cleansing to remove any energy that doesn't belong to me or doesn't serve me for my journey ahead.

This is vital and as I have learnt the hard way, you can't get full access to it until it is given to you by the spirit world. I never take this for granted and I'm humbled and full of gratitude. It saddens me knowing there are beautiful and kind lightworkers out there suffering daily, physically, mentally or spiritually due to selflessly helping heal others and aren't fully protected.

One of my desires whilst I'm on earth is to find a way for all lightworkers who serve spirit in love and light not to become ill. I've seen too many become ill, especially the very gifted ones. At the end of the healing, I'm deep in thought and a little stunned by what has just occurred. I'm amused by my bravery and then shocked by the reality of my decision. Eternity, bloody hell, Jane, yikes!

I come to my own conclusion that whatever happens in the future, I take full responsibility for my decisions. I have a deep inner knowing that the decision had already been made and it was necessary to help others in the future. I have no regrets, fear, or doubts for it all feels pure, loving and right. I'm excited to move onto the next chapter.

GIVE ME A BREAK

After agreeing to allow the Equilibrium beings to surround me for protection, the energy around me feels stronger, more powerful, and I'm struggling with my own thoughts of self-doubt mixed with anxiety. The reason for this is, I've been experiencing relentless healing throughout the night. As soon as I start to drift off, the fun begins.

My upper body is being physically moved into positions more extreme than a contortionist, which should be humanly impossible yet it's happening, and more disturbing in my neck. I couldn't envisage what is happening to me, but I also can't deny the reality for I'm awake experiencing and feeling every intricate, precise move. I ask them why they can't do this when I'm fast asleep, for I don't need to see or witness anymore.

I know all of this is true, I know they have capabilities beyond our simple human understanding, and I also know this can be done quicker without suffering, so why make me watch? "To perhaps write about it," pops into my thoughts. Great, bloody great! I'm tired and to be frank, a little pissed off, for I've shown nothing but dedication.

I remind myself firmly to get a grip for I am lucky to know this process will, at the right time end. I will have full health, balance and peace within not only my physical body, but more importantly, my soul. The pain in my left side is relentless throughout the day to the point I've had to resort to taking painkillers. My left scapular (shoulder blade) feels like it is struggling to stay in position against my rib cage.

It hurts so much I want to rip it off, anything to stop the nauseating constant throbbing pain. The whole of my upper back aches and I feel like an old woman confined to a permanent life of suffering. The left side of my body feels like it is fighting with the right side to find balance. My body wants to be realigned, yet something deep within is not allowing it. My left kneecap feels unstable as though it wants to slide off the knee joint.

Every injury I have had throughout this lifetime, and there have been many, especially in my military days, are rearing their ugly heads. My body is screaming in heightened pain. I can feel energy swirling within my body trying to find balance. The physical body needs to be healed to allow perfect channelling to occur. I have been told by my spirit guides once this process is complete, I will never experience anything like this again.

I repeat these words to myself again and again, drawing strength from these words. I start to question whether all of this is my own fault. Did I not fully cleanse myself after healing another person? I had recently done some healing for a lady in severe pain, with a permanent neck and shoulder injury. The only choice this lady had been offered by medical professionals was extreme surgery.

This lady had come to me I suppose as a last resort before going under the knife. After several sessions, the lady's pain had reduced significantly and only hurt if she forgot about her shoulder and overdid it. This lady was in her later years so was always going to suffer from aches and pains, but she was eternally grateful for she rarely needed her painkillers. Had I stupidly taken on her pain? Had I not fully cleansed myself?

I must have got something wrong, surely? I can't work to heal others if the spirit world expects me to absorb others' pain. I'm no angel, and don't wish to be in pain and misery, absorbing pain from others. No, no, no! Forget that! I was starting to get positive results with my healing that didn't and couldn't scientifically and medically make sense. Professionals could argue it was all a placebo, but I knew and could see what and how I was healing.

Sorry, not how I was healing, but how as part of my spiritual team I was participating. Not only was the whole healing process fascinating and humbling, but blew my mind with the positive results. I was hungry to do more, to help heal the suffering of others, but not at the cost of my own health for that was cruel.

I'm begging my spirit guides to make this stop, or at least return my pain and discomfort to how it was before, make it manageable. I won't moan again; I'll be thankful for my lot. Yes, as you can see, I got myself in a pathetic state. Not my best moment! My Indian guide, with his firm deep brown eyes, appears crystal clear in front of me.

The relief and comfort of his presence makes me want to break down in a sobbing mess. Yet his presence lifts me up with strength and composure. I'm calm and at peace as he tells me this process will take two days. It won't be pleasant, but you will get on with it. The whole process will be complete at the exact right time, it cannot be rushed.

My Indian guide vanishes out of my sight, still, I can feel his presence. Two days, I can do this, I've got this, at least I know it will end. Bloody hell! I must have been an evil bastard in a previous life! The pain continues and so does the relentless swirling within my body. It's like there is a fight going on inside of me, perhaps light and dark.

I can't do anything to ease the situation, so I resort to stepping a little out of the process and decide to learn, watch and gain as much knowledge from the process. I remain hidden in doors for the next couple of days searching for all the positive thoughts I can come up with. Pain means you're alive, Jane, better to feel alive than lose the ability to feel at all! No, that one's not working, I'm not convincing myself.

So, I tried, "Shut up Jane. Two days is nothing!" Please let it be two days. How fantastic it will be to return to my normal, I won't moan again. I remind myself how wonderful my future is, how grateful I am with all the loved ones that surround me. My final thought, my intention is to connect with my divine and sacred healers to complete my healing, now! I hand over my keys (my destiny) to the spirit world.

A strange sensation physically occurs within my soul, I felt something shift, as though I have finally accepted and succumbed to myself. I no longer concern myself with the process, for they have my keys. I trust and I absorb whatever is thrown at me. I will succeed. With this final thought I receive a clear picture of a finish line. Two trees at the end with a ribbon gently attached around each one.

This vision fills me with joy and a stronger

knowing when the time is right, I will be given access to the next chapter. The next chapter without the burden of ill health. The pain and physical manipulations continue as I was told for two days. Finally, the intensity and discomfort settles to the same as before and I'm feeling eternally grateful for I can now clearly see a finish line.

CALMER WATERS

Life feels calmer, dare I say. I'm sleeping better. I haven't been woken up by any curious spirits in the middle of the night, and I'm feeling a little gleeful with all this undisturbed sleep. It's amazing how proper sleep can make everything so much easier to cope with. I've also had very little lucid dreaming.

I'm no longer running around fighting wars in another world. I'm loving it! In fact, life is so peaceful, I start to get concerned that maybe I'm losing my connection and ability to mediumship. Another person comes along my journey who needs help and I quickly discover, to my relief, I haven't lost any of my mediumship or healing gifts. In fact everything is flowing with ease.

That's a relief! I was starting to think perhaps, I was turning into a normal person. Yikes! I'm loving this calmness, or is it the presence of the Equilibrium beings surrounding me with the heightened nothingness? "Don't over think it. Just enjoy it, Jane, for goodness sake!" I remind myself. Each night, I go to sleep intrigued with whether I'll get any visitors but no, nothing.

It's literally as if all spiritual beings, spirits, or energy are forbidden to go anywhere near me. A strong barrier of protection coming from the Equilibrium beings surrounds me. My energy and the energy around me feels different. I feel stronger, more self-assured, and the heightened fear I would often feed off has vanished. I need more time to get used to it. It all feels very foreign from my old energy and what and who I used to be.

I've also noticed my time self-healing and healing others is more fluid. I've finally fully removed my ego. Pure healing, as the loving divine had planned for me to use, is unfolding. Whilst working with spirit, I have always trusted fully in them, but now I trust fully in my capabilities and myself. When and how that changed I have no recollection, but it has changed forever.

I continue my daily practices of cold showers, breath work, and Qi gong to prepare for maximum health for the future. I have seen too many mediums and healers become permanently ill and struggle throughout their lives. They continue to help and channel for others, yet not investing in their own health. If you are going to work for spirit, you must invest in a healthy lifestyle and diet.

I have asked spirit about this several times and

been given the realisation of how disciplined a person working for spirit needs to be. A chosen lightworker shouldn't consume substances including caffeine! Not happy about that one. A lightworker will sense energetically how living things feel, including unfortunately the cruelty of animals. When I thought about it myself it all started to make sense.

If I consumed anything that had been mistreated, including battery fed hens eggs or farmed fish it wouldn't be conducive to my energy or health. I was told by spirit not to consume animals or dairy products, if I wanted to work to the best of my ability, as a pure channel. A medium can touch a piece of jewellery and know all about the previous owner.

Everything about that person, the character, the tragedies, the whole life, so why would I choose to consume the flesh of a living creature? It wasn't until it was explained to me that the penny finally dropped. Please don't get me wrong, I'm not against others doing and eating whatever they want, but for me, I'm not playing in this lifetime and want to be the best channel I can be to fulfil my true purpose.

As I have said before, I'm no angel, and although I have reduced my coffee, I've decided I'm not giving up that pleasure yet. I wasn't planning on writing any of the above, but I was strongly led to. Thought-provoking! Knowledge should be shared, not forced. I hope it helps a fellow lightworker who is struggling with their health. I deviated, so another day has dawned.

I'm feeling optimistic, blimey, sleeping throughout the night is wonderful. My body is full of aches and pains, my balance is still off and I've got this permanent ache in my left eye, but I'm feeling strong. I'm determined to get over that finish line, and when I do, I want my health to be the best it can be. I'm in my front room, standing up, breathing deep, controlled and slow breaths as I follow my Qi gong movements.

Within minutes, I feel the energy in the room become stronger. The nothingness energy fills me with a deep relaxation, as though I don't care. In my peripheral vision, I can see a tall dark figure, wearing a black cloak taller than the height of the ceiling. I immediately know it is an Equilibrium being! I notice the Equilibrium being uncomfortably close to my physical body.

"I thought you were supposed to keep your distance?" I thought annoyed and rather boldly, shocking myself. I'm instantly aware that the proximity is because they need to balance out by energetic/ethereal bodies. My arms suddenly have a mind of their own and elevate out to the sides. The Equilibrium being stood directly behind me with his hands resting on my upper arms. My palms begin to tingle and become incredibly warm.

Without any conscious thought, my head rotates to the left, my mouth opens wide, before I hear an almighty cracking and clonking noise that feels like it is vibrating off my skull. I'm instructed to turn my head back to the front. I can see through my mind's eye the Equilibrium being has placed his painfully thin, grey and very long finger on my neck. He/it has chosen a specific cervical bone, as I can feel he is locating his finger with precision, as his finger moves gently across my spine.

The Equilibrium is sharp and accurate with his touch as I feel beneath his finger an irritated, sore joint that is beginning to pulsate from his touch. I flinch with discomfort as I see a golden laser light go through my cervical bone (neck area) and directly out through the front of my neck to another Equilibrium being who has appeared from nowhere. Throughout the process, I'm fully compliant, calm and trusting.

Instantaneously, I have this bizarre sensation, as though I'm not fully connected to my physical body. My body feels like an old-fashioned wrestling doll, the ones that kids used to stretch into different positions made from stretchy plastic and rubber. My body feels like it is being elongated, stretched beyond human capability.

I'm watching as my body is stretched and pulled. I feel so tall, becoming the same height and size of the freaky tall Equilibrium.

I have the sensation I am taller than the house. Throughout the ordeal, I know the old Jane would have lost the plot and panicked due to fear and run out of the door. It amuses me how I'm so at peace and consumed with the nothingness energy, I can't be bothered to react and have succumbed to the procedure. I won't lie, on reflection, the whole experience is a little eerie!

Eventually, the body is gently stretched up and back down to normal which is repeated three times. Whilst my body is being stretched up and down, I'm given permission to see how the Equilibrium being, standing directly behind me, is manipulating and gently playing with my cervical vertebrae joint (neck joint). I can see he is putting in a blue substance which appears to be moulding around the joint.

He continues to manipulate the blue substance around the joint with perfection. It's fascinating to be given permission to see, not only inside your own body, (a bit gross!), but to see how advanced these beings work. Humans think they are superior but from what I've seen and witnessed, we really are so far behind when it comes to helping and healing one another.

Just an opinion, interesting, if nothing else! As

I continue to watch the area is covered back up, with my skin, before it goes pitch black. I am no longer given access to see any more. My body returns to normal as I'm standing in my lounge, with my eyes fully opened and back in the material world. The Equilibrium beings have distanced themselves further out of my energy, so I can no longer feel their presence.

The nothingness has gone and now I feel emotional, tearful, and humbled that so much dedication has been given to me. Why? I'll only know when the process has been completed. So how do I process what I have shared, how would anyone. The truth is I'm not sure. It feels right and I know it will be to help others in the future. I have to keep it simple and as my guides constantly remind me, I mustn't overanalyse, just get on with it.

Three days pass, I feel different. It's a subtle change of feeling more connected within my body. I feel grounded and strong. There has been no magical cure for my daily physical elements, but I have this inner sensation of strength. I have noticed when I lie down during the day, I haven't been passing out with fatigue. Something has changed, and yes, I believe for the better.

During one of my rest periods, I was visited again by an Equilibrium being. How do I know? The presence of these beings is instantaneous. The vibration of these beings changes the energy, vibration and whole sensation of a room. Sounds a little far-fetched, but it's as if time stands still. There is no breeze, no sound, no material distraction, just a state of formal, serious, nothingness.

It's as though someone more important than a king or queen has walked in. A king or queen you would respect out of manners, morals and because that would be the respectful and right thing to do. When an Equilibrium walks in, you feel honoured, humbled and subservient. I have watched how the sacred and divine healers respond to their presence, and I have witnessed these beings are held in the utmost respect.

I haven't got all the answers, but taking an educated guess, I know these are higher up in the pecking order. What is interesting is, no one fears them, they naturally command respect. I deviated, as agreed they are around me all the time, but only come closer, I have noticed if I need advanced healing or protection. I'm having what I initially thought was a pleasant rest, when the atmosphere changes.

Out of the corner of my eye I can see an Equilibrium standing by my left side. I'm becoming more accepting and intrigued to why I have been honoured by its presence. I can feel myself drift into a peaceful trance of nothingness. I feel so relaxed, safe and tired, I'm going further into what feels like a deep sleep. I'm bathing in pure, peaceful nothingness and feel as though my soul is floating above the service of my physical body, which I find amusing, but once again not in the slightest bit alarmed.

As my spirit is hovering over the top of my physical body, I'm fully aware I'm safely still connected, just slightly detached. My jaw is lifted up and out of the joint and it feels like the front of my skull has shifted forwards making a clunking sound. As quick as it has happened, my spirit returns fully within my physical body and the Equilibrium has disappeared.

I'm lying there thinking that it isn't physiologically possible for the skull, has very little movement and I'm not convinced the jaw has the ability to do that. I remind myself not to overanalyse, it simply is what it is.

A REFRESHING CHANGE

My lucid dreaming has calmed down to the point I'm really enjoying waking up and feeling refreshed. Very little dreams apart from the early hours in the morning before you wake up which I find rather interesting. I have noticed these dreams are frequently related to childlike fears, as though I'm being forced to process and then finally clear.

It can be upsetting, especially if someone you love dies, but then my guides have reassured me this is better and less cruel than this occurring in the material world. You must learn all emotions including heartache, despair, deceit, the list goes on. We will learn all emotions if not in reality, then in our dreams.

Some of us will remember our dreams, others will have no recollection, but I believe we will all receive what we need to learn. Which world is reality, dreams, other dimensions and times or simply this world the one we witness here and now? Perhaps a discussion for another time.

So as not to confuse anyone, this is a lucid dream, or is it? I'm standing with a group of females all dressed in the same, khaki green jumpsuits. We are looking over an airfield. We can see aircraft in the distance, yet it looks unfamiliar. What do I mean by this? I know it is some sort of aircraft, maybe a plane, but I also know it's not. We are not fully permitted to see the aircraft in full detail, to prevent us from sharing our information.

There is no interaction amongst the females. No warmth, no smiles, and it's eerily silent. We are here for one thing only and that is to be tested with our flying abilities. There is absolutely no emotion, vulnerability or weakness expressed with the other females. I stand there emotionless. I stand tall, chest out, and shoulders back.

I am in the military and perceived as a number only and I'm fully aware of this. The strongest survive and the weak are removed. Where do they go? Nobody knows. I know not to show any form of weakness, yet in the pit of my stomach, the fear and heightened apprehension is stirring. There is no choice in this process, we have all been individually selected and our every move is being watched and monitored.

There is very little connection between the female recruits, a mutual respect, nothing else. We have been trained together, live together, eat together, but there is no support for one another. We are forced acquaintances that are highly competitive and simply need to survive. No one is safe, simply a recruit. Numbers which are replaceable. My number is called forward. I'm instructed to sit in the cockpit at the front of the aircraft.

The space is tiny, I'm crunched up in a jockey position, with what looks like a glass lid over the top of me. The space feels claustrophobic as I take a deep breath to relax and take control of my masked, hidden fears. I have never flown any form of aircraft, yet I'm expected to give it a go. I have no choice, but to apply myself fully to the process.

The aircraft suddenly makes a loud noise as I'm hurled into the sky, trying to control what feels like a powerful out of control beast that can't be tamed. I'm controlling the aircraft. How? When did I learn this? Who taught me? I remind myself immediately to stop overanalysing for I know every movement and thought is being monitored.

I continue to fly the aircraft, thinking I'm physically controlling it, yet I have a subtle awareness that my mind and eyes are controlling the movements. The thrill, excitement and adrenaline, is running through my veins filling my body with heightened pleasure, craving for more speed.

I'm exhilarated as my heart is pumping fast

and the adrenaline is rushing around my body. I want more, I need more, I crave to fly longer, as my eyes begin to fatigue and are struggling to process the sensory overload and speed. I feel as though I need glasses or an adjustment to my eyes.

I'm ordered to come down, which I find easy as though I have done this hundreds of times before. When did I know how to do this? And why is it all so natural? As I'm released from the cockpit, I'm instructed back towards the group of women. I notice two have been removed from the group. This is nothing new.

The women are emotionless, fearless and mechanical. There is no sharing of our experiences, nothing. I still have heightened adrenaline pumping through my body, which I know not to share or reveal for my safety. I don't know if any of the others have, as they seem almost vacant and robotic. Their eyes look empty, they have enlarged dark pupils, with barely any coloured iris.

It's as if their spark has died. I'm feeling energetic, full of energy and vitality, and hungry to do it all again. The excitement is short-lived, as I start to question what the hell are we being used for? I then woke up. What the hell. That was so real! Lucid dreams for me are more real than this world! More familiar, strange choice of words.

It feels like I have an understanding and knowing I have lived that life before. Where on earth? I don't know. I reflect on the dream, any truth, substance or reality? It all feels so right. "Blimey," I giggled. I have flown a plane/aircraft, and it was so natural. What has happened and why am I being shown this? I hate the thought of any of this being real, even if in a previous life, but every ounce of my body knows this is not merely a dream.

I also know when others read these books, they too will have experienced the same dreams and have the same deep knowing if they were to be honest. None of this feels right. Are there others out there with the same dreams or flashbacks? I wonder how many ex-military personnel there might be (a mere speculation, no evidence, just a thought!).

So once back in the material world, I need to understand. I thought all that crazy super soldier stuff had finally left me. I had been enjoying my life without the tainted thought of evil, corruption and control of a darker side to manipulate and control man. So why now? I asked my guides and was told as usual not to overanalyse and to keep writing.

I would only be given specific flashbacks to write to help others. I suppose if any goodness is to come out of this, I should just get on and write about it. As I have previously mentioned, I don't just think, I know there are others who are experiencing the same dreams.

Perhaps there is an awakening, truth will always surface to the top, however hard it is hidden. History has proven this time and time again. When will man finally learn that nothing can truly be hidden?

HERE WE GO AGAIN

Well, that will teach me for showing off how wonderful my sleep has become. I have noticed that my lucid dreaming is less frequent, but when it does occur, it always feels more significant. What do I mean by this? I don't question that I have been to these places, for the memories and flashbacks are too strong. I know without a shadow of a doubt I've been to certain places and done things I couldn't conceive.

It's like once you are given several pieces of the jigsaw, you can see the picture/truth being uncovered before your very eyes. The more you witness, you can no longer make excuses, justify, or bury your head in the sand. The dream I am about to share is to clarify there is truth in what others might also be experiencing. What can be done about it, at present very little, but hopefully it will bring comfort that you are not alone.

I felt reluctant to put this dream in, but was guided to. For some of you, this dream will appear boring, but for others, this will be a game-changer to stop questioning yourself. The dream begins. I'm on a remote island in the middle of nowhere. It's cold, damp, and there is a light covering of fine rain, like a veil of transparent mist. The scenery is breathtaking.

There are roaming green hills, lush vibrant trees, and in the distance, I can see mountains with a sprinkle of shimmering snow. The whole military base is surrounded by beautiful, clean and clear, crisp waters. The large lake shimmering in the daylight. The landscape is so perfect and pleasing to the eye, a questioning mind would think it is verging on artificial.

I've been here before several times in my dreams. I always have the same feelings. I don't want to be here and what makes it worse is, I'm separated from my partner as he hasn't got the security clearance. The people are warm, friendly and very engaging. They are very interested in knowing everything about you and are frequently asking questions. They want to make you feel safe, happy, and know that you belong.

The facilities we are all permitted to share are fantastic. The dining area is beautifully set out making you feel at home. The food is of the highest standard, the latest gym facilities, library including café, shopping malls, cinema, it has it all. There is nothing else you could wish for. There are areas where you are introduced to new friends, so no one needs to be left out, or feel any form of questioning why they wouldn't feel happy to be here.

But it doesn't feel right, my gut instinct is screaming, get out! I also know not to share or show any form of disapproval. I've been posted here for at least two years, so I need to keep my head down and play the game. The last time I visited this place, I met a familiar friend I had served with at a base in the material world, the real world. I remember feeling so pleased to see him.

He seemed really pleased to be here, he had completely accepted life on the base. The person I knew before wouldn't have been so trusting and would have questioned everything and been open about it. Perhaps he had his doubts, however knew better than to share them. It was this specific person who had been allocated the job to drive me around to a certain part of the base.

I was taken on a jeep and driven over, I remember clearly a bridge. Beneath the bridge, I could see the choppy freezing cold, clear water from the lake. There is only one way in and out from this part of the island and that is, this bridge. On the other side, I can see there are several buildings. They are all segregated by quite a distance and positioned, so not to be given a full view of what is taking place in each one.

I ask my friend what work is done in those buildings. He cheerfully replies, "Nobody knows, and nobody asks, probably best that way. Everyone gets on and there are some great people here. I'm taking you to the coffee catch up café so you can meet some of the people." Once again, all the people are incredibly friendly, warm and nice. I recognise a few of them, but can't place where I have met them before.

I find myself gravitating to a male colleague with short brown hair, athletic, broad shoulders with strong masculine features. I know him from somewhere, but where? I feel strongly connected and he feels genuine, truthful, and real. As I'm talking to him, his eyes light up as though he remembers clearly who I am. He looks me in the eye and very quietly says, "Play the game, be compliant. Every structure has a weakness, we will find it!"

With this, he rapidly changes the subject, looking a little unsure whether he should have taken the risk to speak so freely. I give him a reassuring look telling him, my lips are sealed. I've woken up, I'm back in the real world. Who was that person? I know him. I gasp as I remember I have seen him appear to me before in a dream, but unfortunately, he had lost his legs.

I shuddered at the thought, I hope he didn't have his legs amputated due to trying to escape. I tell myself to stop making up pieces of the jigsaw. This base does exist somewhere in this world. Whether it is real or artificially simulated is another question. If it is the latter, then the dreams become more tainted, evil and sick. Could humans be used without their consent? Stop it, Jane! This is my friend Becky's speciality, not mine.

Becky, let me explain, is a gifted trance medium; I think of her as a professor of paranormal. She is well connected in the more extreme forms of mediumship, well read, educated and has a vast knowledge on paranormal/extra-terrestrial activities. Becky is lovely, completely normal, and the last person you would expect to be into such a controversial subject.

I quickly remind myself not to overanalyse, just keep writing. That's all my guides want me to do for now. I must be careful with how I word this for I am fully aware I have no proof and it's all speculation. In my younger days, between the ages of seventeen to thirty-three, there were frequent periods of time I would lose. I could be working at my desk then wake up two or three hours later.

I had disappeared, some would say daydreaming, perhaps asleep, but it always felt stranger than that. I would visit certain parts of a unit and know I had been there, yet had no recollection of conversations or memory. I had lost chunks of memory, which I can't simply remember, why?

The truth is, I genuinely don't know, but I'm not a person who would forget details of major chapters in my life!

DRUMMING CIRCLE

Now before I continue, I must make you aware that I'm not constantly experiencing lucid dreams and being visited by spiritual beings. Yes, I do connect to my healing guides when I need to heal or guide someone, but not all the time. I can connect when I want or need to. Otherwise, they are very respectful and understand I also need to live normally in the real world.

My everyday life is the same as everyone else, juggling the demands of teenage kids, being a taxi driver, cooking, cleaning, walking the dog, the list goes on. Not very exciting and doesn't make for good reading. A friend of mine had read one of my books and was fascinated by how interesting my mind worked. I had to explain that these events were what I had felt, seen, sensed and during healing sessions, had participated in.

She knew I was a medium, but still couldn't process the reality of what I was writing. Why should she? It made me chuckle that someone I knew thought that's simply how my mind worked. I'm intrigued why she hadn't run a mile from me. Crikey, if she thought that, I have no change ever conforming or being accepted into society if my identity is revealed. What is it, I'm frequently told? Oh yes, don't overanalyse, just keep writing.

Now I've justified that I'm completely normal like everyone else (although probably only to myself), I shall continue with my journey. My shaman friend has started a Saturday, once a month drumming circle. I am not sure it is for me but I feel it is the right thing to do and go along to support her. I love the drums, but don't fancy being in a room with loads of strangers, especially as I pick up people's energy quickly.

I don't relish the thought of it, but feel I need to experience a drumming circle. I have an inner feeling I'm being directed to go. It's lovely to see my friend and I'm pleased I've made the effort. It's always comforting to go to anything she runs, for she is an experienced shaman, who can cleanse and remove negative energy from a room.

If the room hasn't been cleansed and consists of negative energy, it's not going to be conducive to anyone, however hard we bang our drums. As I look around the room, I can feel myself starting to pick up people's energies, but then have this wonderful sense of strength and control that it's my choice. I shut down everyone's energy infiltrating mine.

Not today and not if I don't wish. I think clearly.

I sense out of the corner of my eye a tall, dark, shadow of an Equilibrium being. It's as though I'm being reminded nothing is allowed access to me unless I give permission. The drumming begins, we are all freely drumming, and the sound of the earthy drums is vibrating through our bodies.

The sound of the drums is very familiar, relaxing, grounding, and comforting. We are all told to stop whilst placing our hand onto our own drum. Breathe in and out, breathing in and slowly out as we call upon a power spirit animal to work with us. I can feel myself go into a light trance, I feel safe and very protected. As I'm breathing deeply and slowly, I see a breathtaking beautiful, strong male lion.

His eyes are staring intensely directly into mine. I'm transfixed at the different shades of earthy light browns, rusty orange, and the depth of his piercing dark pupils that feel like they're drawing me into his soul. I'm reluctant, and decide to draw a little further away from the lion as we are told to begin drumming. The intensity of the room is high, the energy feels powerful.

My cheeks, I can feel, are going red as the whole of my body glows in a comforting, but strong warmth. I can see the Lion vividly through my mind's eye and I hear clearly the words, courage and strength. I also get an instant image of the strength card from the tarot deck. My eye is drawn to a certain part of the card immediately letting me know, strength with gentleness is more powerful.

I feel emotional, blessed and privileged, before removing all emotion and returning into the light trance. As I continue to drum, I can see a large pride of lionesses walking calmly, around and near me, as though blending with my energy. As I'm watching them, I notice and feel the presence of Equilibrium beings walking amongst them. I'm then shown an aggressive, powerful, large lion, hungrily searching for the flesh of his prey to feed his pride.

I sense he is ready to pounce, I am the prey! He snarls, bearing his sharp teeth, and attacks directly towards my face. Just before he makes contact, he hits an invisible shield and falls to the ground. I'm standing there watching all of this and felt nothing, no flinching, no fear, simply nothingness. As I look around, the pride of lions are sat, submissive, and looking at me so gently, as though they are innocent cubs that haven't been taught how to hunt.

The Equilibrium beings are teaching me how protected I am. The drumming is slowing down, letting us know the drumming is shortly going to be stopping. The drumming stops as we go around the room to see who wants to share their experiences. No, thank you. I might not be allowed back again. I decided not to share, and just listen to the others. Everyone in the group had very positive and enlightening experiences (so, nobody nearly got eaten then!).

The drumming starts up again. The drumming fills my body with such a familiar comfort and safety. A safety and connection from a previous life. It feels more familiar than anything I have come across in this lifetime. How can that be, I don't know. The intensity in the room increases as we all continue to drum. I feel so content and relax, I can feel myself going a little further into trance.

I also know not to go fully into trance for this is not the place or time to. I see a black crow, up close, in front of my face. Its piercing, jet black shimmering eye staring directly into my soul. As I'm looking back at the crow, it suddenly multiplies into hundreds and hundreds of crows, literally as though filling the room. I find this strangely comforting because black crows symbolise crow magic, which is powerful.

Crows signify a higher order of right and wrong than laws created in human culture. Crow is an omen of change. Crows can be like everything in life both a positive and negative symbol and is fascinating if you choose to research it. I won't bore you, but it's not as we are led to believe all about death, darkness and negativity. This really couldn't be further than the truth.

Shamanism is regarded as one of the oldest religions and is often associated with indigenous and tribal societies. I'm pretty convinced they knew more about spirit power animals than more conventional religions that followed later. Unfortunately, not all but some beliefs are more dictatorial and less open-minded to the discussion or truth of just how much more exists.

An observation I have noticed is there seems to be well documented healers, prophets, and people who can communicate with the spirit realms throughout history. Yet if you mention a crow, it is immediately for many, related to something dark. My hope for the future is that people will finally think, feel and know what is right for themselves. A human race that doesn't judge, but accepts all on what kind acts they do rather than what a person believes.

Personally, I choose not to belong to any religion for I'm happy with my connection with the loving divine, God, whatever you wish to call it. I find this for me, is a healthier approach for I don't believe in a third party when you can connect directly yourself. Historically often, not always, having a third person can result in abuse of power which we have all heard of. What would the loving divine, God, again whatever you choose to call it, want.

A world consisting of many wars due to different beliefs or simply a world full of kind and loving acts towards one another. Some of the kindest and selfless people I have met believe there is no afterlife, heaven, or anything other than this world. These are the people we should be learning from. Sorry blimey, I really did deviate!

So, I can see literally hundreds of black crows and feel a sense of serenity. I can also feel the closeness of the Equilibrium beings which is heightening the strength of the energy in the room. The beat of the teacher's drum starts to slow down, letting us know we'll be stopping very soon. The drums draw to a silence as once again we are supposed to share our journeys. No way! That's not happening.

I keep my eyes firmly away from the teacher so as not to draw attention and to let her know I'm not sharing. I would freak the group out if I mentioned the whole room was full of black crows and Equilibrium beings that look like death reapers. No, not today! I listen to others' journeys and once again, I'm pleased to hear, they thoroughly enjoyed the experience and had gentle encounters with their spirit power animals.

At the end of the drumming, several of the

people commented on how strong the energy in the room was. I think to myself, if only you all knew! Finally, the last drumming session. We are instructed to ask for a healing spirit animal. The drumming starts and I find myself feeling fragile, overwhelmed, with vulnerability and sadness. The whole vibration around me changes. I can see and sense the Equilibrium beings drawing closer around my energy.

From feeling nothingness, I feel overwhelmed with relief, and love as I see my healing guides draw even closer. I know instinctively I am to receive healing. The whole of my chest, from my throat to the bottom of my pelvis, is bathed in a warm, gentle and loving sensation. I see light within my body as it radiates outwards. I want to break down and weep, for I'm humbled to receive such unconditional love and healing.

I'm distracted by a huge eagle that appears to have flown out of my body. I hear clearly the words, "Freedom, finally freedom!" The beat of the drums slows down drawing the drumming session to an end. "Would anyone like to share their experience with the group?" asked the shaman teacher. "Not today," I thought. I need to get out of here, write down, and process what the hell has just happened.

Before we leave the room, we are all asked to pick a card which will have a specific message on it which should resonate with us. I'm not a fan of this as I think these cards could fit anyone's life if you tried hard enough. I like proof and evidence. I smile, thank the teacher and pick a card. I picked an antelope deer with the words, "You are moving fast now!" I had to admit the connection working with spirit had become stronger and faster.

I smile and chuckle to myself. Still not totally convinced! At the end of the drumming circle, I am approached by a lady who feels heightened stress, sad and fragile. She asks me whether I do readings and then tells me before I have time to answer, all her problems. The poor woman is at breaking point, and I know instinctively a reading would do more damage than good.

I tell her it's not the right time for a reading and that she needs to be kind and gentle with herself. To stop trying to fix everyone and make time to relax and find time for herself. I strongly encourage her that a reading will not fix her problems and potentially make the situation worse. She needed time to heal, for I had already picked up that she had recently lost a loved one.

A card popped into my mind, the tower card which means literally everything around this lady felt as though it was falling apart. She felt she was drowning. One wrong word from a medium/psychic would potentially shatter her if she didn't hear what she was after. She wanted to hear everything was going to be okay, life doesn't always work out that way. I looked at her firmly in the eyes and told her not to have any form of reading.

She needed time to heal, breathe and step back from her life. With these words, she burst into tears and then proceeded to tell me all her problems, which I'm not going to share. This lady had the world upon her shoulders. I just stood there and listened. She continued to pour her heart out and the tears were now flowing freely down her cheeks. At the end, her energy felt lighter although still in turmoil.

She got embarrassed and immediately apologised. I reassured her she wasn't the first and certainly wouldn't be the last and I was honoured she felt safe enough to share her problems. Before leaving, she gave me a huge hug and thanked me. I got into my car and reflected on the day.

At times, I love life for you never know what is going to happen next. That lady didn't need a reading; she just wanted someone to listen to how she was feeling. Listening, by this I mean, really listening, hearing what another person is saying, I believe can create powerful healing.

HOLD IT TOGETHER, JANE

The energy around me feels different. The energy feels stronger, calmer, and more assertive. It will take a little getting used to for I was so comfortable and familiar with my old energy. I've also noticed when I lay down during the day for meditation/trance and healing, the veil between the spirit world and this material world feels thinner.

What do I mean? I know that sounds weird, but it's as if the two worlds are starting to become closer and merging as one. I feel I could almost reach out and touch the other side. I'm no longer sending thoughts up to a higher realm for it feels like inches away from my face. The energy, including the thin veil feels fresher, cleaner and more vibrant.

I'm sure I'm not making perfect sense, so basically what I'm trying to say is everything is becoming more natural and easier, to work with the spirit world. I'm lying down on my bed and giving permission to the higher and divine healers to give me healing. As I lay there going into a gentle meditative state, it feels like I'm within physical touching distance.

I'm reminding myself to stay calm, and if anything touches me physically, not to freak out and lose the connection. The veil between the two worlds feels so fine and delicate like a thin transparent spider's web. The fun begins as my jaw starts to be manipulated and forced into strange end range positions.

The noise is horrendous as bone-on-bone grinding, crunching, and snapping sounds are ricocheting around the room. My shoulders and head are elevated up and forwards. My head is repeatedly flicked to the sides in specific angles, releasing the neck and spine making popping and clicking sounds. My head is then violently shaking, rotating with such force and speed I'm starting to become frightened.

I breathe deeply and reminded myself they have invested too much time in me to harm me. The head is rapidly shaking from side to side as I can feel a warm fluid running down my neck and spine. I'm feeling physically exhausted from all the movement. I can feel myself coming out of the energy, I can't hold the energy any longer. "I'm tired, make it stop!" I shout in my mind. The energy becomes eerily calm.

I'm breathing heavily from all the physical activity as my body lies on the bed, fatigued and still. From the corner of my eye, I see the familiar tall, dark being draped in the black gown. The room has gone from heightened strong energetic energy to calm, and now to nothingness. The Equilibrium being is up close and personal within millimetres from my body. I'm submerged within the being's energy and feel no panic or fear, simply nothingness.

The Equilibrium places his long, thin, pale hands on the top of my head. The touch is powerful, strong yet gentle. The pressure on my head is extreme, as though the weight of my head is becoming too much for my neck to support. I feel this sensation of warmth, prickly pins and needles of electricity that is overwhelming and incredibly pleasant.

The energy from the Equilibrium's hands feels like a fluid of energy running through every vein and cell within my body. My upper body feels like it is being ignited with some sort of light to enable my body to self-heal. The Equilibrium steps back and away from my body. I then notice, much to my relief, one of my healing guides steps in and places his hands on my head.

Beautiful gold light is being administered through the top of my head, down my spine, to my entire body. My whole body feels light, subtly and gently energised and I'm overwhelmed with peace. I feel like I've discovered, and finally found a true belonging and unconditional acceptance of pure love.

I want to crumble to my knees and cry tears of relief and vulnerability as a young child would. I hear myself say." I am no longer a child. I am a strong, powerful woman and will overcome everything." Really, did I just say that? I can see a dark, smoggy shadow gunk, an unhealthy black treacle substance on the left side of my body trying to detach itself from my body.

The substance is attached to the left side of my head, covering my eye, upper shoulder girdle, and heart area. As quickly as it starts to remove from the left side of my body, it returns. Whatever it is, it doesn't want to leave and is putting up a good fight. It feels tainted, dark and evil. Dare I admit, it doesn't feel human. It needs to be freed from within me. I'm wishing it to leave.

My head and neck start to have a mind of their own as my head is aggressively shaken from side to side before being flicked back and forth repeatedly, putting unbearable pressure on my upper neck and spine. I'm being shown glimpses of past lives, memories, and previous war injuries. A fast old-fashioned film of flashing pictures of previous lives I have no recollection of, but yet know they are mine.

The more I see the images, the more I notice this thick gooey, treacle black substance is elevating away from deep within my chest cavity. It's like

I must witness and acknowledge the past events to clear this evil thing from my body. All the hate, fear, death, anger, rage, trauma and guilt held deep within my soul from many lifetimes. The black substance, evil, dark entity is taking pleasure from feeding off all these emotions, I had hidden so well.

Oblivious, I was unaware that I had been willingly feeding this dark thing/creature within. The flashing pictures are ending as I see the black substance finally freed from my soul/body. My chest feels lighter and free, as though I can take a proper full breath of air. All physical movements stop abruptly as I'm lying there speechless. I'm relieved, but also a bit disturbed by what was attached to me.

If I wasn't a hundred percent convinced in previous lives, well, I am now. My mind is blown away by first, the reality of any of this being true, and secondly, how I'd been carrying around so many heavy emotions from other timelines. I had been freely feeding, without knowing a dark substance/entity/thing within. Too much to process! I feel my guides draw closer, which brings me immediate reassurance and comfort that I'm not dealing with all this alone.

They confirm what I have experienced is true, but I'm not to overanalyse, simply write. I can't fully understand or process what happened and agree it would be healthier and better for my mind to continue writing and move on. I do wonder though how many more layers are there that must be removed and how long will it take before I can move onto the next chapter. I send a thought out to the loving divine, "Please let it be in this lifetime."

I'M TAKING A BREAK

I've decided I need to slow down with the writing and take a break. I've become almost obsessive with my commitment to finishing these books. I'm desperate to venture off onto new paths, to do more healing and the occasional reading when it will really help another. I feel frustrated feeling poorly, for I'm a strong character with so much fire, love, and light within me. I'm frustrated by how long the process is taking.

Time is ticking, I'm getting older and can't help thinking so much time is being wasted when I could be putting my healing gifts to help others. I know the answers to all my questions. It's on a time-line, Jane, you will get better at exactly the right time. Yawn, yawn, well I'm bored, annoyed, frustrated and tired. I can't do this anymore (I'm being over dramatic!).

I feel like a caged bird, looking through the bars, desperate to fly free and spread my wings. Hungry to be in my true environment, working in my natural way to fulfil not only my heart/soul, but also my true path. My soul needs to feel alive, working with spirit in the way they have already planned. I need to get onto the next chapter to completely be what and who I am.

I'm not fulfilling my true purpose; I know this, for this light inside is screaming to be let free from this weak shell of a body. I have so much more to do, and yet I wait patiently each day in the hope that Spirit will finally complete the connection of the two worlds, so I won't feel poorly anymore. I have been ensured once the alignment of their side is completed, I will never have to feel like this again.

I know and have seen the future, but I'm also, believe it or not, very logical and still at times question the truth in the words I speak. I've been so focused and working so intensely, I've forgotten it is okay to enjoy the journey. I need to enjoy the simplicity of this life, nature, the sound of birds, make time to meet up with friends, all the things that bring me joy.

I'm at my happiest when I'm in nature, with no other noise apart from the sound of the birds tweeting amongst themselves, the rustle of the leaves in the wind. I bathe in the sensation of all the natural elements, feeling the crisp cold air on my cheeks and the invigorating breeze. When I allow myself the time to submerge myself in nature, properly, no other thoughts, just the simplicity of nature, I feel truly happy and alive.

I spend a lot of time in nature due to walking the dog, but recently I have been rushing back to do more writing or worrying about usually one of the kids. I realise now, I hadn't made time to enjoy the journey. I had become, without realising, a clone of so many others rushing around to what, the grave? Light bulb moment!

I need to reconnect to what feeds my soul – fresh air, nature and no man-made, constant noise. Whilst I wait patiently for the exact timeline for the spirit world to complete what they need to do, I can at least allow myself to spend proper time in nature and breath. It's important for me to enjoy this journey and whatever challenges it brings.

FACE TO FACE

I'm working on spending more time in nature, and it seems to be paying off. I feel more content with my journey, more accepting and less impatient. I'm continuing to work writing and working with spirit but enjoying a healthier balance of life. It's okay for me to put my needs occasionally first. I'm feeling good, rested and relaxed overall with life.

I still make time each day to meditate, for it is vital for my balance and health. I'm still not convinced or own the medical diagnosis, but it helps me function by escaping from the sensory overload of this world. I've adopted along the way the ability to accept whilst meditating/trance, I will only receive what I need.

Nothing more, nothing less, and I'm not perturbed in the slightest by the frequent manipulations and sensations physically moving throughout my body. The fight and fear very rarely exist for I have become appreciative and humbled to receive healing and love that is benefiting me, although be it slowly.

I have come a long way. Seven years ago, I struggled to leave the house due to my brain struggling to balance, repetitive headaches/migraines, blurred vision and heightened sensitivity to noise and light. I must remind myself often how fortunate I am for it is easy to forget how far you have come.

No drugs or treatment from specialists helped, and although I was told not to by my spirit guides, I tried every drug I was recommended. Hence, I became worse until I made the bold decision to listen and trust. The only thing that has genuinely helped me is the frequent visits from Spirit, where I received unconditional love, healing, and a strong, relentless perseverance to get me back on track.

My spirit guides/healers astound me with their commitment. Humans can let you down whether intentionally or not, but I have never to this day been let down by my spirit guides. I have let myself down by not listening or jumping to conclusions in my earlier days, but hand on heart, I have never been let down by my guides. Maybe, just maybe, all of this is on a timeline?

I've noticed it's as though the more accepting I am of the process, the easier it is for my spirit guides to help heal me. I'm feeling happy, accepting and in control, to a point, of my life. Balance, finally a healthy balance of the material and spiritual worlds. I'm doing my daily Qi Gong movements, when the atmosphere in the room changes.

I immediately recognise and can see in my peripheral vision a slender, exceptionally tall dark cloaked figure. It's an Equilibrium being. There is, as always, a sense of nothingness in the room. Nothing, no fear, no panic, nothing! As I see the being drawing closer towards me, I feel nothing but an eerie calmness.

Much to my amusement I find myself continuing with my exercises as though I'm not in the slightest bit bothered that this powerful being is encroaching into my space. The Equilibrium being, stands directly in front of me as it appears to reduce in size to my exact height. It is looking directly at me; I can see red lasers coming out of what I would imagine to be its eyes.

I can't see anything else other than two red, laser lights surrounded by a pitch-black darkness covering its face. I'm staring back, cool, calm and collective, completely unfazed. It's as though the Equilibrium being is gauging my capability and strength. It's analysing every fibre, cell and memory within my body, all within seconds. As I continue to look directly at it, I first notice the eyes changing to its true form.

The eyes are an almost beige/light brown mottled colour. The pupils are like vertical black slits, intense, powerful dark pools of nothingness. I'm mesmerised by the intensity of the pupils as though they are drawing me in, into an endless space and time of another world or galaxy. It's like you would imagine falling into a blackhole in space. I'm given permission to see more of this being's true form.

I notice the skin of the face is a pale, pasty grey, thin in texture, shimmery moist like a fish. As I desperately search to understand what this being is, I get a final glimpse. The face is best described as half human and reptile. I can't fully see the face, yet I already know. Why am I not allowed to fully see the face? Is this to protect the being? I feel for whatever reason, this is correct. The weirdest thing is, I know I have a past connection with this being. When, where, how, I don't know. It all feels so familiar.

As the Equilibrium being draws a little closer, I suddenly feel strong, powerful, and unapologetically just as powerful as it. As I'm connecting with the being, I automatically change my stood-up stance to a wider squat position, so not to be pushed over. My whole demeanour changes from calm to a powerful, righteous warrior. My body feels strange, I have the sensation I have become slightly shorter, stocky, muscular, powerful and fearless.

My body is bare and muscular with patches of sporadic patches of male hair. I'm hunched slightly over like a wild beast, with the capability to pounce if required. I know whatever this thing is, it's not completely human or an animal or anything else. It's a mixture of perhaps, I really don't know, both?   All I know is I feel nothing like my true self!

I stood aggressively, staring at the Equilibrium in front of me, telling it telepathically that I'm not afraid of you and that I'm just as powerful. I feel hostile and aggressive towards it, which is completely out of character, yet I know I must stand my ground. I will show no weakness, for I am equal to this being.

I start to lose connection as I question my behaviour, or am I simply mirroring this Equilibrium's behaviour. "DISCIPLINE!" I hear clearly. I submerge myself fully back into the energy. To my relief, the Equilibrium, as though it has seen enough of my capabilities, draws back and out of my energy. My whole demeanour and physical body returns to normal. "What the hell has just happened?" I asked myself as I took a deep breath.

I feel my healing guides surround me, letting me know I am safe. The tension in my shoulders dissipates, I fully relax as my breathing returns to normal and I feel grounded and back to normal. It feels like a celebration is going on around me. My guides draw close to congratulate me as though I've just passed a very important milestone. My energy is fully cleansed before I'm given permission to return to the material world.

Once fully in the material world, the analytical mind goes into overdrive. What the hell has just happened? I want to go into self-denial, but I can't. I have just blended with an Equilibrium being! I can no longer deny what I am working with.

WHAT HAVE I DONE?

The next few days, I feel awful. My body feels out of sorts, I'm clammy, cold and then hot. It feels like the flow of energy in my body has changed. The lower part of my pelvis feels like it is expanding and there are subtle gurgling noises and a strange sensation of bubbles of air within being moved. Best described as I presume stale, stagnant energy being cleared.

My left eye is in agony, a sharp stabbing, throbbing pain, protruding directly through the pupil constantly throbbing with no let up or release. My balance is off as my brain is working overtime to keep me upright. I'm fatigued, nauseous, and don't know what to do with myself. I retreat to the confinement of my dark, silent bedroom. I feel tearful, frightened, and now I'm questioning myself.

Did I make the right choice allowing the Equilibrium beings into my energy field? Too late now, all I can do is lie here and go with it. No painkillers are working, so I simply have to lie in the dark, stay calm and let it pass. "Please don't let it last too long, make this end, you know I'm happy to work for you," I blurted out aloud. I remind myself not to moan about my previous health ever again and have a reality check how life was just fine, before this challenge.

It takes a couple of days for everything to return to normal. Once I'm thinking clearer, I come to my own conclusion that I'm a good, loving, kind and still the same person. So why did I subject myself to this? The truth, I genuinely believe there must be a reason for the spirit world to invest their time in me.

If I have been chosen to play a small part in putting something loving back into this timeline on earth, I have no right to bury my head in fear. I want to see where all of this is going, whether my visions and what I have been told are true. If I am right, it will benefit all in a loving way. I also decided to question my spiritual guides, and this is what I received:

Why do I feel so ill?

Just hold tight, just a little longer
The blood flow is changing.
Do you know what this means?
The body will have the ability to correct itself.
Sit in the quiet
Watch and observe.
Do not become consumed and low by this event.
For it is positive
It's time for change.
It may become a little unsettling.
But know within

You are at the finish line.
This process will not be pleasant.
But Jane, it will be worth it.
Do not fear.
What you will experience.
For the outcome
Will be one of freedom.
Freedom of the weakness of the flesh
The body is to be restored.
Allowing you to finally work in the way it was intended.
The ability to heal and help others.
More importantly, open the minds of all
This journey will be tough as you have already witnessed.
But the end is near.

So, does this make me feel any better? The answer is, not really, but I have the most precious gift of all, hope!

POOR LOTTIE

I'm feeling thankful for the return of my normal health. When you experience difficult health challenges in life it makes you so much more appreciative of the mundane and the real simple treasures of this life. I love the simple things in life, fresh air, dogs, nature and good, kind loving friends and family. These are the important things in life, not what we are led to believe by social media.

Buy more, bigger houses, expensive cars, designer clothes, more, more, and more. These things are very nice, but the excitement, contentment and gratitude doesn't last long or have the same connection as what I would consider, really important things. One thing that does make life easier is having enough money. I would agree, but craving and striving for more opulence can be a distraction from people, nature, and loved ones around us. More importantly, the passing of time.

So many are consumed by materialism, when those with good health, as the saying goes, health is wealth, are already millionaires. This is so true, but surrounding yourself with loving people or animals is equally important. Whoops deviated, well, I didn't. I was guided to put that in for all of us to stop and reflect. It's been a long day; I'm shattered and looking forward to bed.

I've noticed throughout the day Lottie has been behaving a little more on edge than usual. Lottie, my cavapoo, is such a loving, gentle and incredibly sensitive little girl who picks up human and spiritual energies with ease. I worry about her health, for she senses, feels and knows immediately when energy changes, which I know from experience can be exhausting, if not managed.

As I rest my head on the pillow, the room feels different, strange, icy cold, as though there is an extreme winter's chill in the room. The windows must be open, I get up to check. No, all shut. Lottie starts to pace up and down the room. She wants to get up on the bed to be close to us for protection, but something is forbidding her to come near me. I lie back in bed, relax and go into a light meditation, to see if I can see what is going on.

The frequency and energy of the room feels bizarre. I don't recognise this energy and I'm refused permission to see, which again is unusual. I send out thoughts for protection and immediately reassured by my guides I am safe. Knowing this brings me comfort as I can feel myself go deeper into a light sleep. Tony is lying next to me fast asleep, gently snoring, oblivious to any change of energy in the room.

My jaw starts to have a mind of its own, doing peculiar rotating and end range stretches losing my facial muscles. I feel a sharp, heightened pressure at the back of my head making me feel woozy and a little queasy. I need sleep. I reach over and grab some painkillers to prevent what feels like the start of a nasty headache.

I've got to the stage where as long as I'm protected and safe by my guides, then the process has to continue, but I also need sleep. My jaw is continually being moved now into gentle and dare I say pleasant positions, as I can feel the muscles around my neck and spine being released. I'm going deeper into a sleep, when Lottie frantically starts scratching the kitchen door downstairs.

I get out of bed to check if she needs to go outside to the toilet. The poor thing doesn't know what to do with herself, I can see she is not happy with the energy in the house. However, I also know the energy is for me and won't leave until the process is completed. I pick up Lottie, take her upstairs and put her on the bed.

It's pitch black, 4 a.m. and I'm desperately hoping she will settle. Lottie immediately jumps off the bed and starts frantically searching and scratching doors to find somewhere to hide. I lie there fully awake and come to the realisation there won't be any proper sleep tonight. I decided to put myself into a light meditative state so at least my body will get rest.

I'm lying in the dark as my lower pelvis starts to feel gentle fluttering sensations, as though something is playing with my insides. The intensity of the movements feels bigger and stronger, exactly like when you are in the last stages of pregnancy and the baby is moving and you can feel everything with precision.

I decide to bravely ignore the situation, it goes on and on, as though the muscle fibres and structures within me are being realigned and moved, as though to make some sort of clearing. Access or clearing for what? I don't know. I'm now fully awake and just lying there whilst something is working on my physical internal structures within my pelvis. I try again to get full access to see who or what is working on me, but again I'm denied.

The room is icy cold and the energy is different and unfamiliar to when I work with my spirit guides. I can sense my guides around me, but they have stepped further from my energy to allow this thing in. The energy or being is not an Equilibrium being, but feels on a similar level. A higher, more powerful level. The energy is not threatening or evil but also, I'm not deluded and know it isn't angelic.

The movements within my pelvis start to feel pleasant, as the structures within my pelvis relax and ease off. Every movement feels strong, precise and healing as though scar tissue is becoming more pliable and realigned in a healthier way. My lower pelvis feels calmer, clearer, freer, and less congested. My body feels, strange choice of words, clean.

Eventually it stops, the room temperature returns to normal, and I feel the strong presence of my guides reassure me I'm okay and safe. Lottie appears from nowhere, jumps up onto the bed, snuggles up, and falls fast asleep. I must have fallen asleep as I was startled by the sound of my alarm clock. Tony says, "Jane, what was going on last night, Lottie was freaking out?" So, I gave him a quick summary of what had occurred.

Tony sighed and said, "Lovely. Visited by Aliens again. Nothing unusual then!" I then replied, "It will be worth it in the end, if what I'm told comes true." We then both burst out laughing at how ridiculous our conversation would sound if anyone overheard us. Tony then unperturbed, in the slightest, by what I had just said, went off to work as though nothing had happened.

WHAT THE HELL!

I can't do this anymore. After the last healing session if that is what you want to call it, I feel beaten. My sensitivity to light is unbearable, as though I'm just not designed for this world. I have a constant swirling sensation deep within my body as though my soul is suffocating within this shell. I feel constantly like I'm about to have a full-blown migraine.

"Pull yourself together, Jane." I repetitively keep telling myself. You can do this; you have experienced worse. I'm so tired of this damn journey. The dampened spark within, lights just enough to turn to aggression and anger. I question my guides and tell them I don't believe you anymore, all of this is a load of rubbish! There is no need for me to have to suffer in this way. I know the power, strength and capability you have to help others, so why make me suffer.

Do you want me to crumble to my knees? Is that what you want? Okay, I'm on my knees, now make it stop, please! Silence, no reply, just the closeness of their loving presence, and a loving warmth radiating down my body filling every cell with contentment. This brings me immediate comfort and calmness, yet I still long to hide away, shut all doors and bathe in silence away from this over sensory and stimulating world.

I need freedom to breathe! This world no longer satisfies or brings me joy for it has become a daily battle - arduous, exhausting, repetitive, and frustrating. I know the power of spirit, and that all of this can change within a heartbeat. I then go into a rant about how I'm not doing this journey anymore and I'm cutting off the connection to my guides. These are wasted words, for I know this is impossible as I've previously tried.

The reality is I am part of them as they are part of me. We are one. I'm crying like an inconsolable child, I can't stop crying, I've had enough of feeling constantly awful and pretending to be positive and happy for others. Eventually, I'm so exhausted, I go to bed to sulk and sleep. As I'm drifting off, I can see golden light swirling within and around my eyes, pulsating within and then drawing out.

I'm overwhelmed with the closeness of my guides and feel encased in a warm glow. As waves of warmth frequencies/energies pulsate throughout my entire body. I'm bathing in heavenly bliss of pure love. I'm so content and at peace, my entire body sinks into the bed. I just want to sleep. With one almighty crack, my jaw is lifted out of position and realigned. My face feels sore and tired, whilst my tongue has this strange burning sensation.

I'm nonreactive, and say quietly, "Please just do whatever it is you need to do, quickly." I'm again shown an image of a finish line. I know the final line is near. I also know I have no control of when this happens. I must find a way to fully succumb to the process. I was warned this wouldn't be pleasant, but I could never have imagined how hard it was going to be. I pass out with exhaustion.

As I'm starting to enter a lighter state, I can feel myself pulsating in and out of a light meditation and then desperately trying to remain in the beauty and confinement of the dark nothingness. I'm fighting to remain in the bliss and dark silence where my mind is non reactive to anything. I'm hungry for solitude, escapism of what? My world, the spirit world, myself, and the persistent feeling of not fully connecting to either world completely.

I want to stay in this space and time of nothingness. A safe space where I'm not fully connected to anything. No thoughts, no pushing and driving through arduous challenges, a beautiful nothingness where time, thoughts, physical ailments and a racing inquisitive mind no longer exist. My perfect place of peace, tranquillity and joy. As I lie there, I see out of the corner of my eye, one of my healing guides stepping closer into my energy.

This guide is a powerful historic healer from another previous time. He usually watches from a distance intrigued and fascinated by my progression. Very rarely he will come into my energy but when he does, it reduces you to an emotional mess for his strength of loving healing power infiltrates your whole body with a radiant loving warmth, safety and strength that can't be articulated, for there are no words to describe the honour of his presence.

He stood directly in front of me. I always recognise his hands first, they are clean, gentle, pure, yet all-knowing and strong. Beautifully masculine, but soft and feminine as though he possesses both energies. He wears a pure white robe and smells like you would imagine fresh linen, with a subtle floral smell, crisp, fresh and pure.

The smell is not from this world for it doesn't exist in this time. However, it brings me immediate comfort and calmness. I feel like I can properly fully breathe, for my worries and concerns are no longer mine, and have been taken care of. I get glimpses of his face. His eyes are a mixture of light earthy browns, intense, strong, yet soft and loving. He has olive skin, with strong masculine, handsome facial features. Yet his face appears to glow with kindness and a loving intense warmth.

As he looks directly into my eyes, I know he has already read all my previous lives, and knows every ounce of who and what I am. As I continue to search for as much knowledge on this person, I'm made fully aware to stop searching for validation and evidence. I need to let go and submerge myself into the moment. I'm overcome with peace as though I have completely surrendered. I find myself fixated on his eyes, I forget who I'm supposed to be, and stripped back to an innocent, vulnerable child.

A child who has no concerns or pressures of the material world. A child who sees the world with clarity and simplicity, enjoying the freedom of youth. I feel so safe, I want to cry as I'm engulfed in this invisible energy of loving warmth. My body feels light, non-existent, but I'm still very aware of being in his presence. He holds my hands which I can physically feel before touching gently, the centre of each palm.

Again, I physically hear him say, "The healer needs to be healed first, is this your desire?" I'm unable to speak, I'm humbled, thankful and subservient. I simply nod. Just before he steps back, he places his forehead directly on mine, as my entire body fills with comfort, a powerful love and protection. I start to cry, for I can no longer hold the overwhelming mixture of emotions inside.

He withdraws from my energy and disappears. I'm sobbing like a baby with these hands that have been ignited with a warmth and tingling sensation directly in the middle of my palms. What is it they want from me? As soon as I think these words, I'm overcome with calmness and clarity. I instantly know I now need to make time to blend with my healing guides and perfect the channelling. Why? Perhaps to help others in the future.

I know I need to entwine my energy with my healers to perfect the channelling and have never felt more certain about this decision. My health will improve, as I have been told exactly at the right time, but for now my purpose is to dedicate my time to spirit to perfect our connection, and to write!

TIME TO CATCH MY BREATH

I'm spending more time writing and have a little spring in my stride as I've convinced myself this journey will be over shortly. Deluded, perhaps but I'm feeling optimistic. I've been dedicating specific time during the day to blend with my guides. I had been already doing this, but my feelings towards it have changed. Previously, it was a regimented time slot of focus and discipline, as though I had no choice in it.

A soldier who would simply conform without questioning. Now, I want and need to learn more and have a hunger to understand. A thirst to complete what has been started, because I choose to. I'm on an inner mission to see what I have been chosen to do in this lifetime. The purity and healing love of my healing guide's presence, has opened a spark of brighter light within me.

This all sounds rather self-consuming, me, me, me, but it's really, not. I've been touched by something, I don't like this word but, angelic! Something has shifted deep within my soul that can't be untouched. I'm accepting of whatever is thrown at me and won't falter on this path. Yikes! I have a total of three days of complete inner peace and acceptance. No strange occurrences literally time to blend with the spirit world, write, and breathe.

I'm not deluded. I have noticed a pattern, when things become quiet and mundane, it never lasts. I have taught myself to embrace the quiet times in life, bathe in the moment and be thankful. Life changes all the time. So for those who moan that life is boring, learn to enjoy it for life stands still for no one. I'm sitting in the quiet, going deeper and deeper into a meditative/trance state. I send out a thought to be cleansed of all negative energy that no longer serves me, from previous lives, up until the present.

There are so many layers within each one of us that need cleansing, especially from past times. I was guilty of burying my head in the sand with previous lives, as let's face it, it's hard enough to get your head around this life. Why complicate things with this belief? Unfortunately, I totally agree, but I know from experience with some people they can't get better physically or mentally in this lifetime if their past is embedded deep within them, if left unhealed.

Your choice, what you choose to believe. I initially chose not to believe as I didn't want to comprehend the reality of this being possibly true. It was shown to me several times by the spirit world before I accepted there was some truth in it. Make your own minds up! I'm blending with my spirit guides bathing in the beauty of silence, stillness and nothingness.

A dark green door appears, slightly open suggesting I am welcome to enter. As I walk through the door it is brilliant white. Initially, I can't see anything until I'm greeted by the warm presence of the tall, elegant, beautiful black lady. I immediately relax, for she is familiar and has worked on me before.

There are several other beings present in white clothing and look human. However, I'm not permitted to see their true identity. I'm completely unfazed, for I've learnt to trust this lady over time, and she only ever advances my healing progress. I've also stopped trying to see the other's true identity, for I'm fully aware they will only show me what I can cope with at the right time.

I'm made to lie down on what I presume is some sort of couch. The room, although familiar and welcoming, has the feeling of a sterile, surgical operating theatre. All I can see is people/beings moving around, surrounded by a brilliant white. I'm only permitted to see this black lady's face; the rest is faint and slightly blurry. She is standing to my right-side, towering over me as I can see another being coming closer towards me.

I know this person. He has messy hair and

appears as you would characterise a mad professor of medical science. I have come across him before several times throughout my journey, but never fully allowed to see his face. Maybe that is a good thing? I'm always compliant in his presence which intrigues me too why. Who and what is he? I feel strangely comfortable, relaxed, and knowing he is the best.

I can't feel anything physical, but I am made fully aware he is removing what appears to be a device, a small square computer chip out of my left eye. The chip is placed into a thin small glass tube which is sealed and removed. I ask the lady, "Why hasn't the chip been removed through a funnel? Why have you kept it?" She replies clearly, "To be tested and the information to be downloaded."

Before I have time to ask any more questions, I'm distracted. A surgical tube with a light blue substance/liquid is so bright it lightens up the tube. The tube is inserted in the back of the base of my skull and gently placed with precision and accuracy down the whole length of my spine. I am emotionless. I feel nothing, as I'm watching the procedure as if I've disconnected from my physical body as though protecting my mind from the reality of what I'm witnessing.

The tall black lady by my side instantly knows I need reassurance, as she blends a little closer into my energy bringing immediate love, comfort and confidence that I am completely safe. Telepathically, she tells me my body will now be able to fully heal. The procedure will take a few days to settle. I'm to observe and not to become fearful for my balance will feel off until the physical body adapts.

I calmly walk out of the brilliant white room and head towards the slightly opened door as though nothing has happened. I'm greeted by my healing spiritual guides, but our connection feels different. The connection feels clearer, purer, easier and more heightened as though they have full access to my energy and I to theirs. The connection between us feels lighter as though we are merging into one. Usually, one guide at a time blends with my energy, but I can feel all their energies at once.

Prior to this moment, I would feel nauseous and woozy, unable to cope with more than one guide's energy, but now it feels easy and natural as though we have always had the capability to do this. I feel excited by the prospect of working with my guides again to explore our new capabilities and how we can put them to good use. I'm hungry to push forward onto the next step, but reminded by the words of the tall, elegant, beautiful lady that I'm in for a rough time before things calm down.

Remembering those words, grounds me before I return to the material world. I'm back in the so-called real world. I'm feeling physically fine, but I'm fully aware I'm still buzzing from being in a higher dimension. I start to question myself, could I have just made all of that up? My throat constricts as I'm told off by my guides for doubting and told firmly not to overanalyse and get on with the process.

The spirit world so far has never been wrong and that was including the warning about feeling off-balance. I feel dreadful, but decide to take the emotion out of it and watch as an observer, refusing to fight the healing process and making the situation worse. I hope it passes soon. It will, for everything moves forward.

MIND OVER MATTER

It is exactly three days before my balance and body returns to normal. The energy around me feels heightened as though there is a sense of urgency around me - a window of time and opportunity that needs to be fulfilled. I've not had this feeling before, it feels imminent, serious, as though almost strictly regimented. I remind myself to relax and that I'm in safe hands.

I hand over my keys to my future destiny, to the loving divine accompanied with my gratitude and love. It's pitch black, early hours of the morning, and I'm woken up in severe pain. A sharp metal probe has been inserted up by my coccyx (back passage). I'm frozen in position. I can't breathe. I can feel the blood draining from my cheeks as I feel clammy, faint and nauseous.

I feel like I'm starting to lose consciousness, as I'm drifting in and out of being physically in the room. The pain vanishes as though it hadn't existed. I gingerly move my body, which feels okay. I'm tired, I'll ask my guides in the morning. I'm drifting off to sleep when once more, the sharp stabbing pain again penetrates up through my coccyx (back passage), up throughout the whole length of my spine, to the base of my skull.

The nerve pain is so severe, my whole body locks frozen in position. I can't do anything other than lie there, unable to move, and too frightened to try. I'm begging for them to make this stop, I don't need to witness this, knock me out, please! I can't breathe. The pain is so severe it has literally taken my breath away. I'm starting to feel nauseous.

I desperately want to be sick, but my body has locked as if to prevent the spine from moving, protecting the spinal cord. I have never experienced such nauseating, sharp, severe pain in my entire life. I lie there squeezing my eyes closed tightly, whilst I'm shown through my third eye an image of a long, thin, silver, metal probe the length of my spine being forced like a sharp piercing knife.

It feels like it is repeatedly being rammed up my back passage, touching and manoeuvring every nerve fibre within my spine. I can see the probe is inserted along the length of my spine. The probe looks stationary, not moving, yet there is a frequency pulsating of it, manipulating and gently stimulating all the physiological nerves, fibres and tissues. It's as though the probe is making a clearing space for an energetic funnel.

A straight runway, a clear line of perfection, for what? The answer I already know, I had been told this would occur years ago, but didn't understand the implications, the truth, or the reality of what had to occur. This will be the connection from the spirit world to my physical body. The connection needs to be perfect for the channel worker, not to become poorly both physically and neurologically.

I had also been told that once my physical, mental, spiritual bodies are perfectly realigned, I would never experience headaches, feel off-balance or have any neurological diagnosis. I would, when the time was right, feel, I presume, how a healthy normal person feels on a day-to-day basis. The pain once again vanishes, as though nothing has happened. I take a huge breath and sigh. I can feel my body relaxing and feel so thankful to return to normality.

As I'm lying there, I'm shown a clear image of what looks like a wooden bar across my upper back. Here we go again. Sharp stabbing pain plunges into both shoulder blades causing a horizontal intense excruciating bolt of pain across the upper spine. I'm startled and once again unable to move, let alone breathe. I feel winded with the force of pain across the top of my back which is now radiating down the whole of my spine.

My arms are stretched out as though attached to this wooden structure pushing my rib cage forwards. Within seconds, I'm back to normal, feeling exhausted by the heightened pain accompanied by fear. I'm being shown flashing images of past lives. I don't know the timeline, I sense it could be from the Viking times, but the timelines keep moving. I can see images of a person being strapped to some sort of wooden cross being tortured.

It feels like the person has had their scapulars (shoulder blades) wrenched and torn off, as the physical body can no longer cope with being strapped to the wooden cross. There is a strong stench of blood in the air as I watch on, detached physically from the brutality and beatings inflicted on this person. The barbaric injuries inflicted through lifetimes on this person as though they have been to several wars and fought in battle.

I'm watching a black and white film of another being mutilated, by the venomous, unconceivable cruelty of man. The images are slowing down much to my relief as I realise the harsh reality of what I have just witnessed is in fact, me! This is me being stripped back from all previous injuries and cruelty in past lives or maybe, I could have inflicted on others?

I won't lie, I'm rather horrified with what I have seen, yet strangely, it made sense how potentially we could be responsible for carrying injuries and past memories into this life. Too much, even for me. I need to put this experience into a box and reflect another time when I've finished this chapter first. I like to keep things simple; I console myself with the fact that however awful this journey is to become, I cannot be defeated.

I have been shown my future which I already know I have succeeded. Bloody hell though, really! I still have this impending feeling surrounding me that there is a rush, an emergency to get past a certain timeline. I can't miss this opportunity of progression for this holds the keys to the next chapter.

HANGING OUT DIRTY LAUNDRY

"The Reluctant Medium, part two" book has officially gone live in May 2023. Why am I writing about this? In the hope these feelings will resonate with another and let them know they are not alone. Another strong factor in oversharing is, because I have been told to by my guides. There are many others out there experiencing similar encounters, who in the future will be guided to also share their stories.

It takes a lot of courage to write, even braver to speak openly about other worldly dimensions, energies, spiritual beings and what often occurs physically to certain people. A private person who is considered normal and sound of mind in society doesn't relish the idea of being ridiculed and made to feel like a liar or worse unhinged.

Maybe, just maybe, one person's true story will fascinate and open the minds of all, leading the way for others to speak their truth. A subject that finally intrigues, rather than being mocked due to fear and a lack of understanding. I'm not convinced by many things in this life that people are led to believe. Often, I don't agree, so I always sit on the fence with an open mind, waiting to be proven wrong. I don't ridicule.

I simply come to my own conclusion that certain beliefs are not right for me and I need more evidence. I am a grown, strong woman who finally feels happy and content with who and what I am. Yet releasing that bloody book and all my dirty laundry has made me feel exposed. I feel like a fearful child, vulnerable, fearful, underconfident and anxious.

I continuously remind myself that no one knows who the writer is and to stop this silly behaviour. The problem is I know that in the future, I will possibly need to reveal who I am, to speak honestly and openly to help others. This I have no doubt will come with both positive and negative responses, a mixture of both. I need my health and balance to recover, NOW!

I know I am strong enough to take the blows, I'd rather not, but I need to know that when my time comes, it won't affect my health. I have stipulated to my spirit guides, I will under no circumstances ever reveal who I am until I am completely better. Writing is one thing, but publicly owning your truth is for a real warrior. I'm not feeling it!

I decide to step out of myself and watch as an observer, a technique I've learnt throughout this life. If you can step out of a situation and observe, you really do learn so much more about your behaviour and where it has come from. I have such a deep embedded desire to keep under the radar, and not draw attention to myself. Some people love attention and need the approval of others by posting how wonderful and successful their lives are.

Good for them, I literally can't think of anything worse. I'm not an over-sharer, not that you would believe that by reading these books. The honesty and truth written in these books contradicts how private I am in society. You will only ever see what I allow you to see, unless I dare make a close friendship with you. Anyway, I have identified, like so many others, our adult behaviours often stem from our childhood.

I was a sensitive, quiet, kind child who picked up on everything in the real world as well as the spirit world. I had enough to cope with fitting into both worlds so certainly felt no need to push myself to the forefront. If you met me now, you would not perceive me as quiet, underconfident, or a shrinking flower, but naturally I am. The military taught me how to show no weakness and hide my true self.

I'm thankful for that, for this world doesn't cater to my natural qualities, and I've seen firsthand how those that are perceived as weaker can be easy targets. So, I have this internal battle of feeling naïve and stupid releasing the book and then an inner strength of knowing it was the right thing to do. Then back again to "Jane, why complicate your life and even give the opportunity to others to judge you and form an opinion of you?"

I'm not deluded, if I had read this book, I probably would have questioned the sanity of the writer. So why subject yourself to negative reviews of strangers? Especially the wounded bullies behind keyboards. The simple answer: I must. I've tried so many times to run away and not write these books by deviating off onto other things.

Each time I branch off to do things I find more exciting, than sitting at a computer writing cringe, self-confessing truths, my health deteriorates. I'm always brought back to the keyboard where it is explained by my guides, I will be able to do more practical spiritual healing once I've finished writing. When will I properly learn to fully listen to my spiritual guides?

Who knows, being a logical-minded woman, makes me frequently question this journey. I know it's all true, but what would happen if I completely let go and trusted? I suspect an easier, more fulfilling and healthier journey. I still need just a little more evidence. So, for now, I'll sit back, observe and hopefully, process the inner child fear. You shouldn't suppress feelings, for they can't be hidden forever and will always surface at some point in your life.

I also identify, as much as I would love to be a stronger, more confident, self-believing and in control person, that is not who I am. This I like to look at as being okay, for at least I can resonate with others out there who also struggle. We have all met overly confident, fearless people who strive through life conquering all. I admire their conviction and they intrigue me for they are the opposite of me.

Do I find them warm, endearing and selfless? Not always. Do I find them a little self-obsessed? Maybe a little. Would I want to hang out with them? The truth, most of the time, I must admit, no! So, what can we take from this? It's okay to show and share our insecurities. Most people find listening to just the amazing parts of life a little dull, but hearing a person's truth, however crazy, makes a connection stronger between two people.

Being honest and open allows others to speak from the heart, which is incredibly healing. People who share their flaws, I find more endearing and more interesting. Don't get me wrong, I love hearing how happy and successful people's lives are, but I like to also hear about the in-between bits. I also must mention that everyone, even those who are overly confident, have hidden issues, so never look at another's life as if it is perfect.

Everyone struggles and most have something buried deep within their past whether it be this lifetime or a past lifetime. Some are oblivious and unaware why they feel certain emotions. We all have human flaws, nobody is exempt. So, to anyone who is chosen to walk a similar path or finds life in general difficult, you really are not alone. We learn the most when times are the most challenging.

TOO MUCH INFORMATION?

I'm starting to notice the presence of the Equilibrium being's energy around me more frequently. Sometimes, it is subtle, other times, all of a sudden, I have the sensation I am really tall. I'm a 50-year-old woman and I'm fully aware I'm not about to start sprouting in height, other than perhaps facial hair, but I feel so tall. I'm happily doing my morning Qi Gong when I feel the presence and uncomfortable closeness of an Equilibrium being.

I can see his tall, dark presence resembling a pitch-black shadow. I feel the usual nothingness of its energy making me unable to care or react to its presence. I reminded it, very coolly and calmly, not to get too close. I stress that it is allowed around me, but not in me. As I'm interacting with the Equilibrium, I feel strong and authoritative. I'm setting out the boundaries, and they will be obeyed.

Strangely, I continue to do my Qi Gong exercises as though letting the Equilibrium being, know I'm not fazed by it being there. The Equilibrium being, places his hands on either side of my shoulders. I should be freaking out, yet I'm submerged in the nothingness energy unable to release any human emotions. The hands I notice look old, frail, and the skin is pale with a tinge of grey.

The skin is so thin it has an almost transparent, shimmery texture resembling perhaps a fish/reptile? The hands present themselves as human in structure, but I can't see five digits. I can only see three. Once again, I boldly challenge the Equilibrium being. "Why are you so close? You know the agreement, around me but not within." Silence. The whole room feels of an eerie nothingness.

I'm fully aware it's not within me, I'm very aware, it is encroaching into my energy field. I continue to do my slow, controlled exercises as if letting it know I'm fully in control of how near it is allowed to be near me and setting out clear boundaries. I must admit I like the feeling of the nothingness this Equilibrium being, encases me in, for it quiets the mind and somehow allows you to think clearly with precision, strength and confidence of the mind.

I've never experienced such clarity. My natural reaction to anything like this would result in heightened fear, inducing all sorts of physiological responses. Yet I feel a physiological calmness, no racing heart, fast breathing, my whole body is in a relaxed calm state as though all of this is perfectly natural. I have this inner stillness deep within my soul that feels at peace as though all of this is okay, safe, and right!

My mind is questioning whether this is a healthy response, yet every fibre in my body tells me once again this is right. I have also noticed that since the Equilibrium beings have been surrounding me, my energy levels have increased slightly. I randomly, whilst out walking, suddenly feel incredibly tall. It is the strangest sensation, for I literally feel like I'm seven foot tall and feel cumbersome struggling to put one foot in front of another, so as not to trip.

It is the weirdest sensation, luckily, it doesn't last long. It's like I'm having to adapt to the Equilibrium's energy being around me as it alters my own energy slightly. My energetic field that surrounds my physical body feels like it has been stretched upwards and is still growing. Yikes! I repeat the Equilibrium beings are not in me, but strongly around me. Too much information?

AN INTERESTING CONVERSATION

I'm having a moan to my lovely and very trusted friend, Clarissa. I don't tend to share when I'm really struggling, in fact I usually overcompensate by trying to be more positive and play down how I feel. Just because I feel awful, I don't believe I have a right to drag down the energy of others. There is nothing worse when you meet those people who literally moan about everything and drain the hell out of you.

I also identify there needs to be a healthy balance and it is okay to moan occasionally. Would I want my friends to offload on me? Definitely! I just find it hard to share or show vulnerabilities. Clarissa is different, she has been through a lot of hardships herself and properly understands. I respect her wealth of knowledge and somehow, she allows me to fully let my guard down.

The pain in my left chest has increased and I'm frustrated and complaining why my spirit guides haven't fixed me yet. There's a long silence, and I know Clarissa is tuning into her guide's energy asking for information. "I have already told you, you have the ability to go within and heal yourself. Why haven't you? It will speed up your recovery." said Clarissa. "Yeah, you're right." I replied.

We continue to have a fascinating conversation on what's going on in everyday life, spiritual and mediumship topics mixed in with belly laughs. The openness between us and frank talking, would horrify anyone if they were listening. It is like when we are together, there is no filter. Believe what you want! I have a knowing that I have spent time with Clarissa in a previous life.

I have seen us together as young Native American Indian girls around the age of seven or eight. I could see a couple of teepees in the background and hear running water as though we were near a running river, but I couldn't see it. We are wearing what looks like oversized scruffy dresses playing a game. The game consists of us throwing sticks and stones on the dusty, dry ground and laughing.

We are so relaxed and happy in one another's presence, we could be sisters. There is a strong, fiercely protective bond over each other, as though it is us against the world. When I first met Clarissa, we were complete opposites. Both of us naturally didn't gravitate towards one another, and it took at least a year of sitting in weekly circles before we both allowed one another to see our true selves.

So, on reflection, we were probably more similar.

Both protective of our private lives and only allowed others to see what we wanted them to see. After spirit showed me of our past lives, I have always had a deep knowing that I will always be here for Clarissa in this lifetime. Now, if Clarissa decides to end the friendship, that is her choice. Yet, I will still no matter what, be here for her in this lifetime and hopefully beyond.

The funny thing is as you all know, I'm ex-military, so I'm used to detaching from people and moving on, but with Clarissa it is on a deeper level, spiritual as if the bond can't be broken. I genuinely care and want the very best for Clarissa. Clarissa has told me before to spend more time with my guides healing myself, for some reason, this time, the penny has finally dropped. Her frank words resonated within me deeply.

A moment of clarity to get on with helping myself. I need to put down the writing and spend more time dedicated to caring for myself. I send my thoughts up for my sacred and healing guides to blend with me to teach, guide and show me how I can help heal myself with their aid. Nothing! I usually get something, but again nothing!

I let go of all expectations and hand my complete trust in my guides and decide if nothing else, I'll simply enjoy the solitude of nothing. I'm bathing in the silence, calm and bliss of nothingness going further and further into a meditative/trance state. Finally, I feel the familiar warmth and close presence of my Indian guide. He instructs me to place my hand on the left side of my chest as his hand is gently placed on top.

The gentle, radiating, healing warmth of the chest area runs down my entire body filling my body with tranquillity, calm and love. I want this sensation to last forever, and time to stand still, for I am completely at peace. Another guide steps in, his energy more intense and serious. This guide is a surgeon. He works with precision and advanced techniques and technology, which as unhinged as this sounds, hasn't been discovered in this timeline on earth.

He shows me inside my left eye, where I can see an inflamed, enlarged, red and irritated blood vessel attached to what looks like a vein. I continue to watch on as this guide inserts a long, sharp needle into the inflamed angry area. I felt nothing, but watched in fascination, knowing not to move. Within the needle is a blue substance that is injected into the irritated area.

I'm made fully aware there is nothing structurally wrong with the eye, simply the inflammation needs to be removed for the eye to heal. As the liquid is administered, I can see the area calm down, the structures, tissues, veins all returning to a healthy colour and the swelling disappearing. I feel another guide step in who I have named Blue. why? Because the energy all around him is blue and he takes down inflammation within the body for others, I have worked on.

His job is literally to remove inflammation throughout the body and allow the body to heal quickly with minimum discomfort. I started thinking, "Interesting, I wasn't expecting that." "STOP, JANE!" I hear the firm, disciplined, strong, male voice of my Indian guide. I immediately submerge myself back into trance, letting go fully of my human emotions and thoughts. I have been given permission to watch and learn, but no thoughts or emotions are to weaken or hinder the process.

Almost twenty years of strict, disciplined methods of mediumship finally paid off for something! I'm blending with my healing guides as I'm trying to steer the healing back to the pain in my chest. Nothing! The connection has weakened. They are teaching me I am part of the process, but not the leader. Got it! I go back into trance and simply bathe in the energy. Again, the silence, stillness and inner peace I'm experiencing is pure bliss.

I can feel every muscle fibre relax as though it is pliable plasticine, sinking into the ground.

I've lost all awareness and drifted off. I'm woken to a physically sharp, plunging and stinging pain directly into my left breast area. My head automatically tilts over to the right side. My head goes numb and feels peculiar, as if an anaesthetic needle has been injected into the sheath of skin between the skull.

The fun begins when my head is forced aggressively into once again over to the right stretching the muscles of the neck on the opposite side. I'm fully out of trance, and trying to stay calm and relaxed. I'm using every relaxation technique I know, breathing slowly to aid the process. The pain is excruciating, and I'm struggling to maintain a calm composure and let the body heal itself.

As this is occurring, I'm being shown flashbacks of images of upsetting memories I thought I had overcome, healed, and put to bed. Obviously not. I observe my logical brain is fine with my past, but my muscle fibre memory has held onto the raw emotion. My chest area screams in pain, as though years of past life turmoil are attached to my heart. My mind accepts, but my body is unable to let go.

More flashbacks, some I recognise, others I don't recall. Guilt, shame, sadness, anger and heartache are all buried deep within every fibre of my body, particularly my chest. More and more flashbacks, previous miscarriages and the guilt, pain and a sense of failure, as my physical body let me down to provide a safe, secure environment for my babies. I'm watching this with an eerie calmness, no tears, just amused and then shocked by the still raw presence of hurt.

The wound, still after all this time, weeping in sadness and deep pain. There is no sign of the area healing, just an open, angry, and exposed heart-wrenching pain, as if a spear has been plunged deep within the heart. The flashbacks settle down and I return to the stillness of the here and now. I fully cleanse, disconnect and thank my guides.

I remain sat in contemplation and a realisation that although my mind is accepting and forgiving, my body has held onto the deep emotional pain. My body needs to grieve and heal. How do I do this? How can I help myself fully heal? Even more complicated, how do I free and heal myself from past life trauma? Bloody hell, is nothing straightforward? As much as I want to rush through the healing process, the reality is as my guides have told me all along. I will be fully healed at exactly the right time on the right timeline!

Back to the drawing board. Looks like more time to sit in silence and blend with my guides to be shown with them how to fully heal. To listen fully to my guides and what my body is trying to tell me. Time not only to listen but to really hear!

A LESSON I MUST LEARN TO PROGRESS FORWARDS

I've been continuing to do healing on others that spirit engineer onto my path. It fascinates me how they literally materialise from nowhere. I'm being taught by my guides to only heal those who ask, and I mustn't volunteer. When I hear someone is in pain or needs healing, I have a natural desire to offer my help. Spirit has instructed me, I must be asked, then check I have consent from my healing team.

I have this internal battle with myself, to just listen and keep my mouth shut. One of my close friend's children was ill, and I was overcome with desire to help her child in any way I could. She didn't ask, I pleaded with my guides to get her to ask for help, yet she didn't. I felt awful, guilty, and mean not helping her child, but was instructed under no circumstances was I to interfere unless my friend asked.

Her child was getting worse and ended up in hospital. I couldn't take standing back and doing nothing, so I connected with spirit to ensure the child would be okay. I was told the child would make a full recovery in time. I didn't intervene, perhaps a little bit, but just to find out my friend's child would be okay. The lesson I'm being taught is, I can't heal everyone, nor should I try.

The healer will burn out if she doesn't listen to her guides. I am part of a team, not the leader. A moral dilemma, but once you step out of the situation, it makes perfect sense. I ask myself, if my spirit team had told me about a different outcome for my friend's child, would I have obeyed? The truth, probably not! I would have done anything to have helped that child.

Wrong answer, totally but as I have said all along, they could have picked someone more compliant. I am now fully aware, not to offer my services unless contacted and asked. I have been asked by others to do distance healing for the very ill who do not believe in what I do. I first check with my spiritual healing team if I'm allowed. If I'm given permission to heal, I tell the person who has asked, to get the person who needs healing, to ask me.

I need permission from the person. Some could argue I could ask their subconscious. This is correct, but only to be used with those who can't communicate fully or animals. I would literally spend all my time healing others and not get this book finished. Spirit knows this and that is why they have put boundaries on my time. So in between writing this book, I'm contacted to do healing for people who require extreme methods. I've noticed a pattern.

People don't come to me for a gentle Reiki chakra cleansing. It seems to be complex. Dark past trauma from both this lifetime and past lifetimes. I have no idea what to expect when I go to heal another, other than I'm one hundred percent guided, shown exactly what to do and protected. This makes me laugh as if anyone had told me eight years ago, I would be working in this way, I would have run a mile.

Fascinating what once would have petrified me, no longer bothers me. I won't lie, sometimes what I see questions my analytical mind for I had no comprehension any of this could be real, yet I'm okay with it. How and when did this occur? Through years of gentle teaching and guidance from my team. I've been contacted by mediums that are closed off to receiving healing from others, which I suppose is a compliment.

These healing sessions have been the most extreme and complex to date which I am unable to reveal out of loyalty to these very private people. A true lightworker's energy, a person who has been chosen by spirit, and not necessarily initially wanted to walk this path. I have noticed it can be repeatedly sabotaged by darker entities.

It's as though as the person becomes more selfless in helping others and healing/

mediumship abilities increase, the dark side becomes more intrigued by their energy. The dark side will try to prevent the lightworker from putting light back into this world. I appreciate this sounds ridiculous, but it's the truth. I also know this will offend some readers that believe healing is all about the intention you send out.

Send out love and healing and that will protect you. I love this beautiful, loving thought, and I want to agree with you as that would be my desire for this lifetime, but I can't. This is not to scare anyone for fear feeds darkness, and I have no intention to frighten anyone. I cannot lie and simplify working with energies as all airy fairy and light.

In the same token this doesn't happen to everyone, and it tends to be those who have been chosen to serve as lightworkers. There are lots of people who choose to work in healing methods, but not many who are chosen. Hopefully, this will reduce any worry. For those who have been chosen, spirit will give you the right protection at the right time on your journey. Ask for protection!

AN ANGEL IS SENT MY WAY

I'm on the phone to my very good friend Becky or as I think of her, the professor of paranormal activity and untold truths. As we are chatting away, Becky mentions her close friend who is a very gifted and talented healer. Becky has mentioned her before and suggests I should contact her for she has vast healing abilities including removing past life traumas and dark energies. I've never felt drawn to have healing from her.

"Becky, she won't be able to heal me for I'm constantly told by my spirit guides I will only be healed at exactly the right timeline by them. I would love for someone to come in, heal and fix me, but that is not how it is going to happen." I told her. As I said the last few words, my throat starts to constrict, making me fully aware there is some substance in what Becky is saying. I wonder, should I contact this lady?

As soon as I've finished speaking to Becky, I need to find out what is going on. I have a knowing I need to contact this lady. I confirm my feelings and accuracy by writing. When I need to clarify something for myself, I find this takes the emotion and any self-doubt or questioning thoughts out of the situation and makes it more official. I'm told there will be an exchange of healing. We will help one another.

Interesting! Didn't see this one coming. I'm intrigued and fascinated to see what the spirit world has engineered. I get the details of the healer from Becky and see a photo of her. As soon as I see a photo of the healer, I'm instantly filled with calmness, kindness, loving and gentle energy. This lady is the real deal, selfless and handpicked to heal from above. We arranged a Zoom call!

The Zoom call begins, and I'm blown away by the gentle, healing calmness of this beautiful woman. She has wisdom gathered over hundreds of previous lives including from Egyptian times. She has an advanced knowledge of how to work with all energies. She is a true healer who puts the well-being and safety of others first, over her own.

I'm truly, genuinely fascinated to be in the presence of this lady for I have never experienced the purity, kindness and selflessness of another, anything remotely like this. She also has this powerful strength around her that feels subtle, but lets you know this is not a woman to be messed with. She also understands the importance of time.

What do I mean? We are here to do good,

help others, and put back love, positivity and healing whilst we are here. She is humble, not materialistic or craving validation or any form of appreciation for her dedication in helping others. She is simply here to do her job, touch and heal the hearts of as many people's journeys before returning onto the next life (heaven, another dimension, whatever you choose to believe in, that brings you comfort).

I'm blown away by her sincerity and her ability not to have brought into the material crap and hunger for celebrity status. She serves the sacred, divine source with love and compassion in her heart with no ego. The first and only person I have met with no ego! I wouldn't have believed it, if I hadn't had the honour of being in her presence. I'm humbled!

I feel so calm and knowing in her presence. There is no awkwardness, just a genuine intrigue in how one another works. The strangest thing is we already know about each other as if we are reading one another's souls. As we both dig deeper, we are discovering one another's true essence of why we are here and what each other's true purpose is. I now understand why she endlessly gives and is a true mothering figure and nurturer of all.

It's fascinating as we talk freely, drawing out and picking up on private details and heartfelt experiences of each other. Speaking freely, honestly and openly as though both are comfortable to show our true selves. Both of us are incredibly private, however for some reason the barriers have been removed for each of us to know what we are entering into.

I will only reveal what was picked up for me and that was, as I had been already told, I was almost at the finish line and just needed the final adjustments and tweaks. Her words, "The spirit world has been working to perfect and realign you. The final outcome will be like a line of dominos, one stacked in front of another in a perfect line." In my mind's eye, I could see the dominos going down my spine.

A perfect channel for the spirit world to use me to heal others. She continued, "At the moment, the dominos are almost there but look more like fish bones crossing over one another but in a zigzag formation. There isn't much work left, it is just down to fine tweaking." As she expressed her findings, shudders of chills and energy ran through my body confirming her words to be true.

She then asked me what I thought was going to happen to us meeting and perhaps working in some form together. I explained I had already been told I would receive healing from her that would make me feel more settled, calm and happy with the process ahead. Her healing would aid me to the finish line at the exact timeline. I would also need to heal her if she would agree, as my spirit guides had made me fully aware of what she needed.

I explained in detail what and why she needed healing which she confirmed was correct. This lady was so gifted, she had experienced a lifetime of attacks by dark energies, in the hope of stopping her from shining her light to help others. This lady had fought on where others would have run and hid. I could see several occurrences within my mind, it has been brutal. How did she remain so loving, kind, and giving?

I also knew she would have gone to the depths of despair, which made her more compassionate. Her body felt tired, painful, and I knew every day the shell, her body would feel like a constant battle, yet her soul shone so brightly. I felt passionately it was her time to receive healing, not necessarily mine and hopefully, good would come from us working with each other.

As our conversation continued, the healer laughed and mentioned I wasn't what she was expecting. I jokingly commented that I hoped that was a compliment, but knew what she meant. I come across as full of energy, relatable, a little too free with my tongue that makes people laugh, feel good about themselves and then out of nowhere, they share their hidden feelings.

I'm nothing that you would imagine, to be working spiritually. Sometimes, someone will share something they hadn't thought about for years, buried away and tried to forget about. Anyway, it is times like this that I love being me and feel so thankful that spirit allows this to take place. When another person shares a strong past or present memory that they hadn't planned to share, I feel genuinely honoured. You get to witness healing before your eyes.

I deviate, more to the point I could have spent hours talking to this lady. Her energy made me feel so calm and knowing everything would be okay. To be in her presence was like bathing in a calm tempered lake, surrounded by a forest of natural beauty. A stillness within my soul and a gentleness in my heart. No other disturbance of human emotions, just a calmness and inner peace.

She feels unearthly, angelic and beautifully pure. I know that if ever this healer reads these words, she would be mortified, but that's because she can't see herself as others do, which makes her even more special. Our conversation ends. The healer agrees to spend time on healing me and when the time is right, I will heal her. Wow! Again, I didn't see this coming.

My mind is blown by the meeting of this

lady. The funny thing is, we both identified our meeting had been engineered at exactly the right time by the spirit world. The power and higher intelligence of the spirit world never fails to fascinate and blow my mind. So, what will happen? I don't know but it feels good, right, so I'm going for it!

THE HEALING TIME HAS ARRIVED

Today I will be receiving a distance healing. A distance healing session, for those who might not know, is receiving healing from a distance. The healer is not physically in the room when they are sending healing. A person can be in another country, town, or city. Energy healing has no boundaries. Look it up, if you are interested as I don't want to bore you.

I prefer doing distance healing myself as it allows you to go into a deeper state with your healing guides and the freedom to move without toning it down, so as not to disturb the client. A time is arranged, the person receiving healing is sat or lying down in a quiet room where there will be no distractions. The healing session usually lasts for thirty to sixty minutes, but there are no set times because it is led by the healing spirit team.

Once the healer has finished, she/he will contact the person via text. If the person receiving the healing wants to discuss the process, time is made to talk over what has taken place and how the person feels. Every healer works differently, however that's my experience and a simple explanation. So, before I receive healing, I choose to sit in the quiet and blend with my spiritual guides and ask them to give this healer full permission to aid my journey and healing.

As soon as the connection is made, the atmosphere and intensity is one of seriousness and I'm surrounded by a stronger energy of pressure around me. It's 10.00 a.m., the session is to begin. I'm sitting in this already intense energy as extra pressure is applied to my head, feeling like it has been put in a vice. I can feel waves of gentle pressure throughout my skull. My head naturally wants to rotate looking over my left shoulder, so I go with it.

I can feel my eyes pulsating, and different waves of warmth as though very gently releasing the pent-up tension behind and in my eyes. My head feels so heavy and fatigued. I'm struggling to hold my head up right. Out of nowhere, I see a clear image of an old-fashioned picture of Jesus. I'm not a fan of religion, yet I feel comforted by this image.

The energy around me feels thicker, heavier, and denser than what I normally work in, but I understand it needs to be for the healer to gain access to my physical body. The healer, I identified, was working between the middle and higher world which she had perfected with years of healing. Working within different dimensions when used for good is a selfless act and not without risks, the healer needs to have full protection around them.

When working in the higher world, you are more protected. Working in the middle world is denser, like treacle and potentially more at risk if not fully protected. I can hear the outrage of those who believe all healing is about love and light and your intention. Yes, correct, but there are so many different layers to healing and we all have different experiences and paths to follow.

I found it fascinating observing, feeling, and knowing this healer's techniques, trusting fully in her spirit team and selflessness. As the healing continued, I could feel a beautiful healing warmth deep within my chest area. A pleasant radiating warmth in my upper back as though she was physically standing behind me with her hands on my shoulders.

A warm fluid ran from the base of my skull down the full length of my spine, as though the fluid within and around my spine needed to move more healthier and free. I could feel the healing ending. I sat there so relaxed as I'm shown a perfect black and white baby scan picture. As I'm watching this scan picture, it is rocking from side to side, as I realise my body is also slightly swaying.

The heightened sensation of love fills my whole body with pure peace. I can see this baby is attached to the left side of my chest and needs removing. I feel no desire or rush for it to be released, as though it is buried so deep within my soul it has become part of me. I continue to watch the image of the baby scan picture rocking and swaying within my left side. I say within my mind clearly, "It is time to go. It is safe now for you to go."

The image is detached from my chest, and I see a funnel of air which removes the baby out and away from my chest into the right time, space where it belongs. I feel a gentle sadness mixed with relief, for this energy was draining my energy and not allowing me to move forwards. For the child, I feel a calmness, joy and contentment that the energy is where it truly belongs. "Enough!" I hear clearly from my guide.

The healing has finished, but I can still feel this incredible and comforting heat within my chest and body which feels strangely mothering. I feel safe and content at this precise moment, and don't want to fully break the connection. I decide to break the connection, eager to know what and if the healer discovered anything. I check my phone.

There is a text, which I hadn't heard from the healer asking if I would like to discuss the healing. Yes, please! I'm greeted by such a calm, gentle and loving voice, exactly how you would imagine a healer to sound. When she speaks, you feel cocooned in a safe bubble of safety. I told her I tried very hard not to see as a medium, but admitted I saw quite a lot. Only what spirit permitted.

She asked what I had experienced, so I went on to explain all the physical sensations and the truth of what I had seen. Before she explained what she had experienced, she asked me if I was comfortable with past lives, as not everyone is. Totally! Yes, please. She explained she had to do a soul retrieval.

A soul retrieval, for those who might not know, is an ancient shamanic technique that finds lost parts of your soul that you might have lost due to a traumatic past, lost, or ill-health from this life or a past life (research it if you are interested). She also explained she needed to remove an attachment. So, what did she find?

Here goes. She went on to explain I was a natural healer, surrounded by a beautiful green energy, and that it was my birthright to heal. I had to heal others. In a previous life, in the early stages of New England, roughly 1620, I was born to my mother who was a very gifted healer. In those times, it would have been very dangerous to have been discovered as a healer for this was considered evil and witchcraft.

Unfortunately, my mother was born with a

healing gift so strong and powerful, it was discovered. There was a knock at my mother's door, which was the authorities, and the child, which was me, was snatched out of my screaming mother's arms and taken away. The mother was tortured with metal devices and hanged.

The healer explained she wasn't given permission to see what happened to the baby. The heartache and despair of the mother losing her child had resulted in her searching for her child throughout future lifetimes. She would not rest until she had found her stolen child. Through pure grit and determination, she searched through many a lifetime until she eventually was reunited with her child, me!

Her love for her child was so deeply embedded, she refused to ever be parted. The healer had to gently explain to the mother it was her time to return to where she needed to be. That she had done a good job protecting her child, but now she needed to return, for it was healthier and the right thing to do for her child.

The mother eventually agreed and was detached from my chest through a funnel of air to the right timeline, and finally could rest in peace. This had occurred when I saw the image of the baby, but I had no idea it was my mother. The healer explained this was one of the reasons why

I felt drained of energy and was unable to fully heal.

All of this I sounded farfetched, yet felt right, honest, and was confirmed by my guides as the truth. It shouldn't have made sense, but it made perfect sense. Throughout this lifetime, I have a very close bond with my mum to the point at the age of seventeen, I couldn't bear being parted from her and the thought of losing her was unbearable. I made the choice at seventeen to join the military.

I needed to leave the safety of my mum so I could survive without her, even though I didn't want to. I had this inner unhealthy attachment to my mum that I have never discussed with anyone, and knew I had to break free. Everything made complete sense to me, my behaviour, and a secret inner detachment anxiety that I had carried from birth. One of those lightbulb moments!

The healer suggested it would be nice to perhaps light a candle in memory of my mother to reassure her she was still in my thoughts and our bond of love could never be broken. I was not to connect with her too often, so she could rest knowing she had done a good job protecting me, but now needed peace. The conversation came to an end, and I sensed we were both intrigued by where this journey was going to take us.

The healer would contact me again when she

was told by her spirit guides, I was ready to be healed again. I appreciated this, as I only heal when I am given permission by my spirit team, when the exact time is right. Neither of us work on demand. We work when told. So, did I light that candle?

Yes, I did, and I thanked her from the bottom of my heart for being such a loving and protective mother. I reassured her our bond would never be broken, for you can't sever love and she needed to enjoy the inner peace she had rightly earned.

Well, I wasn't expecting anything like that. On reflection, all of it made sense on my behaviour in this lifetime. I found the story very sad, for a mother to spend lifetimes in heartache and pain, but then felt joyous she had finally found peace and healing.

LIFE CONTINUES

After the last healing, unfortunately my health regresses. I feel this constant nauseous imbalance running throughout my body, as though swaying on a rough ferry crossing. I've become intolerant to light and sound, knowing full well this is a time to remain calm, hibernate, and go with it. I remind myself, what did I expect if I just had an attachment removed from my body.

I hang onto the hope that one day, all of this will be a thing of the past and I will feel so well, I will struggle to remember this chapter. I can physically feel my body trying to recalibrate the imbalance from within. It feels like a constant battle of energy swaying within, fighting for peace and equilibrium. I wonder if it could be me not allowing myself to fully heal? I try to do some writing, but I feel too poorly to work.

I resort to simply sitting in the quiet, meditating deeply to escape this damn shell of my body. It takes four days for my senses and body to finally settle back to normal. My mum makes a reassuring comment on my health, "Jane, why can't you stop doing these silly spiritual things, and maybe you will get better on your own."

I must admit from her perspective this would make sense. Bless her, yet not what I wanted to hear.

"Mum, we have already had this conversation. I've explained the outcome, it's something I have to go through to get better." I spoke. "Just saying you were getting better until you messed around with that spiritual stuff," said Mum. "OK mum, maybe you're right, but I've started this journey now, and I'm going to see it through," I told her.

My mum has this inner desire for me to see the error of my ways, and like an unruly sheep, return to her proper flock, the church! Her intentions are pure, loving and coming from a good place and it makes her happy.

HOLIDAY TIME

I'm so excited we are finally going on holiday to Greece, Kefalonia. I'm so looking forward to escaping from the mundane. No writing, cleaning, cooking, taxing kids around, or healing for others. I'm so excited I just want to explore the beautiful Island, drink coffee whilst people watching and spend quality time with the family.

We arrived in Kefalonia and it's breathtakingly beautiful. Our villa is in a quiet part of the island, surrounded by luscious greenery, mountain views, overlooking the crisp dreamy light blue sea. Standing outside the villa, I feel the weight upon my shoulders melt away as I take a deep breath of happiness, gratitude, and pure relaxation. We can't wait to get inside, what looks like a pretty picturesque and well cared for villa.

As soon as I walk through the front door, my throat constricts, telling me there is energy in the apartment that shouldn't be there. Bloody hell, really. I'm on holiday! I don't say a word. The bottom of the villa feels okay, although I can sense it is not right, but not threatening. As I walk up the top of the stairs, I shudder as my blood runs cold. There is one specific area where the energy feels eerily cold, and I find myself wanting to step around the space.

"Really. I'm supposed to be on holiday," I hear myself talking to my guides. I console myself with the fact it will be trapped energy, nothing I haven't done before, and I'll get rid of it when Tony takes the kids out. I decide not to breathe a word and jollily get everyone excited by how nice the villa is and how lucky we are to be here. The energy feels unusually strong, intense and powerful, with a mixture of sadness and heightened fear.

I tell myself off, not to presume until I have the villa to myself where I can find out properly what needs removing. Finally, we are unpacked and sat outside admiring the beautiful views. One of my children asks me if they can have a quick word. "Mum, I don't like it in the villa, there is a man staring at me, you need to get rid of it. It feels sad and scary," said one of the kids.

"I will, I'll speak to your father and get him to take you all out tomorrow so I can cleanse the apartment. For goodness sake, don't tell and scare the other two, please." I pleaded. I reassured her it was fine, not threatening, and I would cleanse her room before bed. First thing tomorrow, I would investigate. I can't do it now as everyone is shattered from the journey.

We all sat outside, having a drink and something to eat enjoying the warmth of the last few rays of sunlight. Out of the corner of my eye, to my right, I see a large grey and white male wolf. He is so close, within touching distance. The wolf's strong, intense, piercing eyes staring directly at me. That's interesting and a little disturbing, I won't lie. So I ask my guides why I am shown this image.

I'm told not to worry. I'm completely protected and so is my family. I already know wolf symbolises strong protection and would not come to you unless you requested the appearance of one of the tribe's greatest teachers. I was once told by my shaman teacher you cannot pick wolf; wolf picks you. Once a wolf picks you, he will protect you for life and where there is one wolf, there is always a pack.

So, putting two and two together, I presume I'm about to learn something, whether I want to or not. I console myself with the wolf's presence, knowing we are all protected. I very rarely see spiritual animals, as I don't ask to see or choose to work that way, so it was intriguing and caught me off-guard. It's times like this I'm so thankful for the knowledge I have learnt on my journey. Otherwise, I dread to think how I would have reacted.

What is it they say, knowledge dispels fear!

Not totally convinced by this. I prefer we are only taught in this life what we can handle. I couldn't have coped with any form of shaman practises a few years ago, for I was still fearful of the unknown. Whilst we are all chatting and laughing outside, it fills me with such pleasure seeing everyone relax and enjoy themselves. I have a secret dread of having to sleep in the villa tonight, but will sort it out in the morning.

Lying in bed, I feel like a fearful five-year-old child scared of the dark. I'm anxious, my heart keeps fluttering, and I'm sensing lots of sadness, fear and chaos lingering in the atmosphere. Every time I'm just about to fall asleep, I see this crazy middle-aged woman with mousey brown curly hair waving her arms around at the bottom of my bed desperately seeking my attention.

"Stop this, Jane! This is not your fear!" I repeat to myself. I call in protection knowing I am fully safe and no harm can come to any of us. The sensation of fear is erratic, out of control, and I'm struggling to compartmentalise the energy. This lady is relentless and is too close for comfort. I ask her to step away, but she is having none of it. "Get a grip, Jane!" I repeatedly tell myself. I don't sleep a wink, it's awful, and even in the presence of my guides, I can't stop feeling on edge.

As soon as Tony wakes up, I explain there is an unpleasant energy in the villa and I need him to take the kids out so I can deal with it. "Bloody hell Jane! Really, we are supposed to be on holiday!" Tony said. I then confessed that one of the children was frightened due to the energy and he immediately agreed to take the children out. Just before they left, I caught the other two children whispering outside.

I asked them what they were whispering about, and they confessed they didn't like the villa for it felt strange, but didn't want to say anything in case it upset us, as we had spent so much money on it. The energy in the villa was stronger than I thought, for everyone apart from Tony, could sense something was wrong. My lovely Tony, with his no-nonsense common sense and practical mind that could work out an answer for everything.

Sometimes, I long for his practical approach to this life for it is so much less exhausting and straightforward. I like the difference and the balance we bring to one another's world. We are opposites, but then similar in our basic views of how we value and treat others, ourselves, animals, nature and we value time and experiences more than material items. He was the only one who slept peacefully throughout that night.

The same child who initially picked up there was something wrong with the apartment came storming into my bedroom and started freaking out. "Mum, I felt sorry for whatever it is in the villa, as they felt so sad. Well, I don't now as it's nasty, aggressive, and feels evil. I haven't slept all night as it's been looming over me and scaring the hell out of me. Mum, its eyes are bloodshot, and they don't look human, please get rid of it, I can't sleep," said one of the kids.

"Stop panicking, there is nothing that can harm you. I've spoken to dad, get ready quickly and he'll take you out," I said. I won't lie, I'm not feeling comfortable with the thought of investigating whatever is in the apartment, for it feels like whatever it is, its feeding of extreme uncontrollable fear, terror, and mayhem. This energy is turning whatever it is feeding off, into evil darkness.

The energy I know doesn't want me in this villa and will increase its intensity and behaviour in the hope of us leaving. Out of nowhere, all my fear dissipates as I feel anger towards this thing. How dare this energy frighten my children! It's okay to come for me, but not for my kids. Bring it on! I feel an overbearing protective strength, like a lioness protecting her cubs. I'm going in, you don't mess with my family!

Tony takes the kids out to explore the local area, we agree I will text him when I'm finished. I'm sitting downstairs in the lounge, having a frantic chat with my guides, having a little moan that they know I don't like working this way. Removing energies, especially not nice ones, is better suited to people who like the adrenaline and thrill. That I can assure you is not me! But, I also know it is morally the right thing to do.

I feel overcome with a strange sense, I'm suffocating, drowning, gasping for breath. My chest feels heavy, as though something is physically pressing against my chest as though not allowing me to stand up from the chair. It's strong, incredibly powerful and trying to stop me from working. Calmness overcomes me as I feel the intensity of my guides surround me as my throat constricts reassuring me, I'm never alone. I'm fully aware there can be no doubt.

I must commit one hundred percent to what I'm about to submerge myself into. I take slow, deep breaths as I go deeper and deeper into trance. The presence of my guides is so serious and strong, it is verging on uncomfortably warm, but also empowering. Silence, calm, nothingness, and then I feel the presence of Medicine man.

Medicine man appears when dark energy needs removing so I know it is my responsibility to keep the energy perfect for him to work through, including with me. As I stand up to walk towards the bottom of the stairs, I feel fearless, hungry and passionate, as though excited to go into battle.

My body is swirling within as I'm allowing Medicine man to take the lead. I'm filled with an almost arrogance, authority, and strength so powerful, it is screaming loud and clear we are here to win. I'm feeling untouchable, heightened power of over confidence as though doubt never existed. As we come to the top of the stairs the energy changes, it becomes softer, gentler and more loving.

Medicine man steps back out of my energy as a divine healer, enters my energy. I feel blown away with the sensation of purity, divine love, and safety. I feel like a humble child, not worthy to be in his presence. I'm given permission to use my mediumship skills to see what is in front of us. I first see frightened children clinging onto their parents and grandparent's hands.

Communities of people huddled together gasping, short of breath, and reassuring one another, it will be okay. The love, care and gentleness of these good, kind people, all showing consideration for each other. Babies frantically being carried with cloths over their faces protecting them from the dirt and smokey air. Thousands and thousands of people are trapped, as if suffocating in a trapped time.

Their heightened fear, anxiety and desperation is tangible in the atmosphere. I'm shocked by what I'm witnessing and overcome with sad emotions and feel motherly and overprotective. "Concentrate, discipline!" I hear it loud and clear. I'm here to help, not become consumed, straight back into trance. The healer stands closely by my side, filling my whole body with calmness, peace and pure love.

He creates a funnel of what looks like a white light of air. The healer directs the people towards the light swirling funnel, ensuring them they will be safe, loved, and looked after. They all recognise him, trust him, and don't question. Thousands of people all obliging without question, trusting in this one healer. There is no fear, just a quiet happy sense of peace. A peace I have never felt so strongly or ever witnessed before.

The energy starts to feel a little frantic, as if there is a rush to get these people through the funnel. Medicine man appears to my right and I can see him refusing entry to some of the people/souls. These souls you can see have a slightly different colour around them like a rustic orangey, brown red. It is easy to identify these souls are slightly different and not as pure as the others.

They are not permitted to use the same, light funnel of the gentle, loving, kind souls. Medicine man directs these people to a different area that looks like some sort of segregated pen. They are being kept away from the others to ensure the safety of the others. The funnel feels like it is weakening. I can see all my healing guides step in a circle formation around the funnel using all the strength and energy to keep the funnel open.

I can see other light beings surrounding them as more and more light beings gather. There seems to be hundreds of light beings that I can't fully see, yet look like light orbs. I don't know any of them, but their energy feels mighty, powerful, pure and healing. The energy feels peaceful and calm, but there is a knowing we haven't got much time to ensure all these people return to their true home/time.

I've never seen so many people go through a light funnel of air. I'm not exaggerating, I'm talking thousands! We continue to gather them up gently, constantly reassuring them they are safe, and going into the loving light. Once again, not one person questions the healer who guides them. Finally, every single person is safely returned to where they should be, home. The funnel vanishes into nothing.

No rest, there is a seriousness and urgency in the air. The divine healer steps out of my energy as Medicine man steps in. As medicine man draws into my energy, the inside of my body starts swirling, as though there is a funnel of air running the entire length of my body. I automatically start making these strange, deep, breathing noises like you might imagine a tribal didgeridoo.

Another funnel appears to my left where the remaining rusty orangey, brown red looking souls are located. There is no one there gently reassuring them to go through the funnel. It was more of a disciplined, formal command. I noticed the funnel was a different colour, more of an earthy dimmer colour. The funnel didn't go directly upwards like the previous funnel, but more to the side as though to a different time and dimension, to perhaps be rehabilitated?

I genuinely don't know, but they certainly weren't allowed near the purer souls. The mission appears to be complete, yet it is vital we check over the entire area. A small innocent brown-haired boy, no more than seven or eight is huddled up, sitting on the floor with his head bowed down between his legs. He appears frightened so we cautiously and gently get a little closer.

Medicine man orders me to stop, as he creates a funnel. Medicine man reveals the identity of the innocent, frightened child. It is not a child or a human soul, it is pure evil, dark, menacing, and demonic. Medicine man engulfs the energy, before aggressively forcing it into the funnel. Again, the funnel swirls off into a different direction before vanishing.

Finally, I feel myself take a deep breath and start to come down from high alert. However, the energy doesn't feel settled. My eyes have a mind of their own as they start rotating from side to side, frantically searching as though hunting for prey. The whole atmosphere feels dense like wading through a bog of mud in a dark forest with no light or way out.

Medicine man starts to increase our energy as though gearing up for a fight. Our energy is expanding larger and larger as though we are bigger than the whole villa. I feel stronger and more powerful than I would imagine a lion before he pounces on his prey. No doubt, no fear, just a hunger to succeed in battle. I feel, if there is such a thing, as power itself!

I sense and then see peripherally the Equilibrium beings draw close around me. Just close enough to protect, but not enough to participate. I sense they are watching and analysing how I cope with the situation. I feel the whole of my healing team drawing closely into my energy heightening the sense of strength and power around me.

Behind my healing guides, I get a glimpse of what looks like a mixture of shamans, tribal beings, and other light beings that I don't recognise. My eyes continue to rotate frantically from side to side searching for what? Suddenly my eyes abruptly halt as I look directly in front of me. A large smog of a shadow substance heads directly over the top of my head, surrounding my entire body, as though trying to engulf and suffocate me.

I can't make out its true appearance, but I can see its piercing dark black, bloodshot eyes that look frantic, wild, and blood-thirsty, as though ready to pounce. It's not human or an animal, it's from the depths of darkness itself. A darkness one can't envisage for this is so dark and evil there is no flicker of light within. It is part of Satan! From hell!

I feel detached, no fear, calmly analysing its every move as though strategically gaining a military advantage. There is no doubt in my mind I have already won the battle. I automatically know what to do as I raise my hands directly towards the dark smog, pushing it further away from me. As we push it further away, I can see Medicine man has created a swirling dark smoggy funnel to the right of me.

I continue to push this evil darkness towards the funnel. The fight is on, the strength of this dark, evil thing is powerful. As hard as I'm pushing, it's not budging. Still, I feel no fear, just a determination to succeed. A courage and inner strength I couldn't have imagined. The light and dark energies seem to be of equal strength. We have a standoff!

I can see more and more light beings standing behind me. There appears to be hundreds of them all directing their energy towards and through me to defeat this evil, dark creature. We expand our bright golden energy larger and larger, as I notice we are creating a transparent shield which looks like a bubble. The shield is to stop any of this darkness infiltrating our light.

We push and push against evil itself, as I start to breathe in and out in a deep erratic way making strange, high pitched, screaming sounds. Sounds that don't belong in this world. Sounds that are only recognised in the depths of darkness and evil. Screeching, violent, and aggressive noises, forbidden for humans and light beings to hear.

It feels like eternity as we push again and again whilst screaming these horrendous, unworldly, raging, violent, and wildly aggressive high-pitched sounds of an unknown language towards this demonic creature. Finally, the fight looks like it's going in the right direction as the large smog of dark shadow begins to dissolve into a smaller substance. The swirling dark funnel sucks it away.

The whole atmosphere changes from mayhem to calmness and peace as though nothing has occurred. There is a joyous, happiness of celebration in the air filling my entire body with euphoria. As I stand silently and bewildered on the top of the stairs, I'm shown sprinkles of golden light like fine rain drops covering the whole villa and the entire part of the island.

As I'm standing watching, I can see glimpses of blue light mixed within the gold rain drops of light as though healing the entire island. I know instantly that what has just happened, has healed this land of its past. As I'm still standing there, I'm overcome with waves of blissful love and happiness, as my entire body bathes in the rain of light as though being cleansed myself. Suddenly, everything returns to normal.

I'm still standing there amused and a little startled by the reality of what I have just witnessed. I quickly pull myself together and discipline myself to fully check I am cleansed and protected. I walk downstairs, sit in the silence as I send my intention for full cleansing and protection. Within seconds, I'm back in the spirit world greeted with a joyous celebration of congratulations and loving warmth.

I notice first my Indian guide bowing his head before noticing the others are doing the same. They are implying I am now fully in charge. I ask them not to do that, as we work as a team, as one. They are my strength and comfort. I don't want to be in charge yet. I'm happy with how we have been working. They assure me they will continue to support me, but I now must take full control of my power.

I'm no longer a child, but a woman of strength, courage and power. I'm feeling a little amused, before I notice a door open in front of me. I know the door is for me as they only appear when I'm given permission. I walk through the door as I'm greeted by the sight of a familiar face. It's the tall, elegant and very beautiful black lady. Her energy is so loving and pure I always feel safe and comfortable.

I also know the room is full of other beings but appreciate I'm not given access to see them.
"Well done, you have completed stage three. Not many people get to this stage. Your body will need to adapt, and unfortunately, you will feel unwell. This will all settle down and pass," she says gently. I'm lying down on what appears to be a white table, surrounded by brilliant white everywhere.

I can sense and feel several beings in the room moving around, but the brilliant whiteness hides their appearance and the surroundings. As I lie there, I have a sensation and knowing my energy is being cleansed of any impurities. I see a large needle inserted into my left arm where I can see a blue liquid injected. "What is it you have injected into me and why?" I asked. The black lady calmly responds with, "You cannot work to the level you are working in without help. Your physical body can't cope with it."

"This is to ensure you can physiologically cope and work in the levels you will be expected to work in. This substance will protect you physically and prevent you from becoming ill. It is impossible not to become ill working at this level without it." I take the opportunity to ask for more healing and realignment of my physical body. I hear clearly from the lady, "It has been granted."

As I continue to lie there in a peaceful meditative state, I see what looks like a dark silver, metal, robotic, thick creepy centipede inserted in the base of my skull. I'm calmly watching some sort of device crawl down my spine. I'm shown the damaged area in my cervical/neck. The inflamed and damaged tissues surrounding the spine are being eaten up, removed and repaired by this thing!

The once damaged tissue around and within the vertebrae somehow is regenerating itself with healthy pink tissue. Where once the disc between the vertebrae was compressed and worn down to very little, suddenly it is becoming spongier looking, larger and healthy. The disc between the vertebrae of the neck area no longer looks compressed, normal in size like the other discs.

I'm then told this device will stay within my body until all the surrounding tissues are repaired. A bit gross, I won't lie! Am I bothered? No! Should I be bothered? Yes, probably. I have got to the stage in this journey where I'm genuinely not perturbed by any of this farfetched, sci-fi fictional, or perhaps true advanced technology. I no longer allow my analytical mind to race away with fearful thoughts. It is what it is.

Does it feel right, good, pure and for a better outcome, one to do good in the future? Yes! That's good enough for me. I have learnt to have a simplistic approach to all of this and that is, I know all of this is very real, but I will sit on the fence until I have proper evidence. The evidence I need is to make a full physical recovery to fully believe in all of this. Harsh on my part, yes, but logical.

I have witnessed such advanced technology and things that in this world would be seriously ridiculed and laughed at. I feel privileged, however I need to see proven facts. Where unfortunately at the moment all of this would be interpreted as fiction. The process comes to an end, I return through the door to my healing guides before fully returning to the material world. I'm sitting there thinking this is getting ridiculous.

I know what has happened is true, but really! Did I just participate in removing dark, evil energy? I didn't sign up for this. The thing that amuses me the most is where and how I suddenly become all courageous and brave. I'm so perplexed by the whole experience, I decide to put it in a box, lock the key, and maybe, revisit it at another time. I'm on holiday, I am going to enjoy myself, and hopefully, there will be no more funny stuff in this villa.

BREATHING SPACE

Tony and the kids return full of energy and laughter having had a lovely time shopping, drinking coffee and eating ice-cream. "How did it go, Mum? Have you got rid of it?" said one of the kids. "How does it feel? Feel for yourself," I answered. "It feels normal, different, nicer, but proof's in the pudding for tonight. We'll see if you are any good then." She laughs, never fully convinced by what I can do.

Much to my relief, we have no more episodes of strange occurrences taking place in the villa. It's good to see everyone using the whole of the villa rather than congregating permanently outside. The next few days I have noticed an increase in my energy, but unfortunately, my balance and spatial awareness feels slightly off. Strange choice of words, It feels like I'm floating within my brain as though a sea of fluid is trying to find equilibrium.

I feel aloft, not fully connected within my body. I remind myself I should be feeling pissed off for didn't I just do something selfless, rather irresponsible for thousands of strangers trapped in time. Perhaps I deserve a health break! Gosh, that would be nice, yet surprisingly I'm accepting. I was told my symptoms would get worse, until my physical body adapts to the process. It's not like I haven't been told this would occur. I'm taking a breather.

I'm on holiday and calmly observing as though silently detached emotionally from what I am feeling. It's like I'm watching a scientific experiment on someone else, intrigued by the outcome. Something significant has changed. After seeing those frightened souls return to where they belong, it has put my insignificant worries into perspective.

I've been walking blindly in this lifetime, consumed by what we are led to believe that the here and now only exists. The reality is there are so many layers upon layers of different dimensions and yes, other energies. I can't fully process what I've witnessed and nor do I have the brain capacity or desire.

I feel different, I feel humble, thankful and eager when I am chosen to work again to help those who the spirit world choose me to work with. After writing those words, I have a little chuckle, for this resembles nothing of the apprehensive woman scared of a few human spirits lurking in the dark. Blimey, how time has changed me!

GIVE ME A BREAK!

The holiday continues and there are no further energy disturbances within the villa, much to the kid's delight. It's wonderful watching everyone relax, laugh and really enjoy themselves. I have to decline going out with the family in the next couple of days due to an increase in vestibular migraines. Did I previously mention I felt accepting of the journey, and was calmly watching from a distance?

Changed my mind. I'm feeling frustrated, a little bitter towards the spirit world. I thought after rescuing hundreds of souls, doing morally the right thing, maybe, just maybe, I would be struck down with a bolt of lightning, a miracle of healing powers. No! instead, I'm rewarded by going up another spiritual level of feeling like shit! Sorry folks, I forgot I was spiritual! For a moment.

Oh well, in for a penny, in for a pound. I'm far too committed now. You might have guessed I'm wallowing in a little self-indulgent pity for myself. Well, I am supposed to be on holiday. Really! Oh, the joys of this journey. I remind the spirit world, I know their true power of healing and that I feel it's cruel and unkind to subject me to this suffering. The problem is as I know, this is simply part of the process.

Shut up Jane! Stop moaning! You've got this and won't be defeated. Moan over, I'm back in the game. I make a determined decision, whatever is thrown at me, I will not be beaten. I have seen the finish line and it's my god-forsaken right. Tomorrow will be better, and everything moves on.

I suddenly remember out of nowhere, my good friend Eddie once telling me, this lifetime is an illusion. I send thoughts out to be shown and taught how to break through this illusion of perpetual hardship.

BACK HOME

Well, gosh, what a relaxing holiday, I feel amazing! Well, that's how I imagined I would feel. Unfortunately, I'm hiding indoors due to the persistent feeling of a migraine trying to fully bloom. My left ear is screaming in pain as though I have an ear infection. I'm shattered. My eyes are struggling to maintain my balance and the surrounding movements of everyday life. I decided to write, for I need to understand.

I'm told the usual: the cause is due to increasing the energy between the two worlds. My physical body must learn to adapt to the new level. Wait for it! I have had a device placed within my ear to enhance my hearing spiritually which will not be pleasant but will pass. I am not to become fearful but sit in the quiet, observe, and remain calm, knowing this will pass.

After admitting to this, I really think in the future it would be sensible not to declare myself as the writer! Decision made now, I feel comfortable to continue writing. I have a confession, why not, as I'm officially back in hiding from embracing my truth. I have always, since a child, been able to see spirit, sense and know spiritual occurrences, and on occasion, have been able to hear spirit physically.

What do I mean physically? Not simply by thought but as though, someone is talking, as if physically in the room. Hearing physically is my weakest discipline, which I put down to fear as I'm not overly keen on hearing, as I find it rather creepy. At this precise moment in time, I'm past caring. Just get on with it. I'll deal with the hearing when it is perfected.

A couple of weeks pass before my health returns to normal. Normal! I really don't know what that word means. Out of the blue, I received a text from the very gifted healing lady asking if I would like some healing. Yes, please! We arrange a time and date for a distance healing session.

THE HEALING SESSION

I received a text to confirm I am ready to receive healing, at the time we had previously agreed. I'm sitting in my lounge, bathing in the silence. No one in the house, just pure silence. I have a firm word with myself to submerge myself into the healing, and not watch what and how the healer is working. I am to merely sit and receive healing with love and gratitude.

As I'm sitting there, I can feel my entire body being bathed in a beautiful warmth, as though I am being hugged gently. I can feel the protection and presence of my spirit guides surrounding me. Knowing this, I drop all barriers. I'm tired, I don't want to see the process, for I'm just grateful to receive. The intensity of the healing feels stronger than before. I experience a pulsating, gentle, vibrating and bubbling energy running up and down my body.

I'm shown an image of an old-fashioned radio, implying spirit is working on my frequency. I can see and feel what looks like waves of frequencies going within, up and down, inside my head. I used to experience this a lot as a child. As a child, this used to frighten me as it felt strange. The best way to describe this is, for those old enough, an old fashioned black and white TV.

When the final programme had finished, the screen would go all fuzzy, before you would turn it off. That fuzzy screen would feel like it was inside my body. I would feel strange and overcome with nausea, until it was turned off. Fortunately, my body has adapted to this sensation, and I find it quite pleasant. Probably helps that I'm no longer frightened by it, in fact, I find it fascinating. Not nice for a child though!

As the healing continues, the waves running through my head feel smoother, as though the frequency is becoming clearer. I can see the once black and white fuzzy screen has become a softer and calmer light beige/brown colour. It feels calmer. I would even say it is feeling pleasant and reassuring.

I remember as a child, I would become so overwhelmed with this awful nauseous pit of fear in my tiny stomach. I would force myself out of the energy and scream the house down. My poor parents. A child, three to four years old hasn't got the words to articulate what they are experiencing.

As I'm bathing in the sensation, the frequency starts to run up and down my entire body, as though realigning my spine. My eyes begin to flicker as a beautiful green light shines directly into my left eye. As my eyes begin to settle, the green light continues to work throughout my head, gently moving over to the right side. I can feel warmth and the gentle touch of fingers, as though massaging my face at specific points.

This gentle touch is loving and pure. I feel so precious, special and loved by the dedication and determination of this energy. This healing energy is balancing the left and right side of my brain and eyes. This sounds ridiculous, but I'm overcome with pure love, gratitude and humbleness.

I don't want this sensation to stop, for I'm encased in love and protection, as though cocooned in a sacred womb. I'm pain-free, blissfully happy, content, and loved! I'm overcome with a sense of euphoria, and feel blessed to have had the honour to receive such pure, healing energy. I have no doubts about what has just happened. I have received divine healing.

The healing ends. I'm sitting there quietly absorbing what has just taken place. I have no right to doubt my path. I cannot falter, as I am surrounded by something way more powerful than me, and I will get over that finish line as I've already seen. The healer contacts me and we discuss what each of us felt and witnessed. She informs me another door has been opened.

This is the final door, it is open, but I'm not

ready yet to walk through it. I informed her I had already been told this on holiday and then I spoke freely and honestly to what had happened on holiday. No holding back, I trusted this lady, and knew she could cope with soul rescues for I knew she had experienced similar encounters.

As I explained in detail the soul rescues and the darker energies, I used the word "evil." She stopped me in midtrack, and said that she was pleased I had used that word, for so many believe we only work with love and light. This can't be true for one can't exist without another.

To help another person to heal, it can require removing an element of darkness from around, within, or attached to them. I would like to think a true healer wants to heal. How can you heal if you aren't brave enough to remove darkness that is stopping a person from healing? My opinion only, thought-provoking if nothing else!

We then went on to have a further conversation on this subject, which confirmed what I had learnt along my journey was correct. This conversation was honest, open, truthful and I gained further knowledge which I'm eternally grateful for. I once believed in love and light and I still do, I simply know sometimes, you must remove the not so bright energy away so love and light can shine brighter.

THE VEIL IS THINNING

After the healing session, I take the next few days slowly. My body needs time to adjust. I've noticed first thing in the morning, there is more pressure in my head as though my head is in some sort of vice. I can feel a migraine coming on. Whilst my head feels like it is in a weird vice contraption, I know a migraine is strangely forbidden to escalate.

This is unpleasant, I feel bloody awful, but I find this oddly reassuring. My brain is finally taking back some form of control. I choose to calmly observe how my body will respond to this. It's not long before I find myself back in the bedroom, blinds down and lying there desperate to escape the world.

I reach over to the bedside cabinet to grab some painkillers, but just before I take them, I'm told to stop. I know I need to see how my body reacts without intervention. What is it they say, the body can heal itself. I love the idea of this, I desperately want this to be the case, yet once again, I need to experience this for myself. As I lie there, I send up my intention to receive healing from my sacred and divine healers.

I'm in a state of deep relaxation, silence, and a beautiful nothingness. I'm bathing in the pure bliss and stillness of nothing. No thoughts, nothing. My throat gently starts to constrict, as I feel a gentle web-like substance touching the top and left side of my head. I'm surrounded by my healing guides that instantly fills me with joy and contentment.

I'm clearly shown the beautiful black lady step closer into my energy, I feel completely safe and protected, my entire body surrenders. Her presence feels stronger and closer than previously. She is standing to my left as I can see her place her hands over the left side of my body. I'm told not to move. My jaw starts to have a mind of its own as it is forced into different and unusual end range positions, making loud clunking and cracking sounds.

I find myself noticing, although my head and neck are being manipulated, my whole body from the neck down is perfectly still. There are waves of warm energy flowing down my body into my lower pelvis; however, my body is perfectly still. The energy feels different, everything feels closer. The veil between me and her feels thinner.

It feels so thin, we could physically touch one another. It's as though our two worlds, dimensions, I don't know the correct terminology, are merging into one. How could this be? A reality of perhaps the two worlds merging as one. I hadn't ever thought this could be possible, but now my mind is open to endless possibilities. The healing ends. I'm analysing as I lay there, the realisation of what I've just witnessed.

I could feel the physical presence of this lady, even the change in gentle air that surrounded her every move. As the day progressed, still no full-blown migraine, but extreme pain in my chest and sternum as though my rib cage was being moved with delicate precision. I'm intrigued and I feel optimistic that as the veil becomes thinner between our two worlds, I will be fully healed.

I also know that once fully healed, I will have developed my healing gifts to their full potential to relieve others of their physical pain. This fills me with excitement, for so many are suffering without the chance to fully recover. On reflection, I chuckle at the old Jane seven years ago, who would have been petrified by this experience. The spirit world is so clever.

They have taught me at exactly the right time, each step of the way how I am stronger, braver, and more capable than I think. That last sentence is for each one of you reading this book! Today I still struggle as everyone else does, but I understand fully the importance of time and just how precious it is.

Time is not to waste on self-doubt and fear. At fifty, you become aware that we are not here very long. I'm not here to play at any of this, I'm here to complete this chapter and work in however the spirit world has chosen for me. I'm not out of the woods yet, it's going to be physically and mentally challenging, but I'm strong. Bring it on!

NEVER DOUBT SPIRIT

I initially decided not to mention what I'm about to reveal, but have been strongly guided to by my guides. Why? I don't know and feel a little awkward too, here goes. Whilst on holiday, Tony was really struggling with constant headaches. The headaches started directly after a vaccination, and he tried everything to get rid of it. This had gone on for over a year, and he'd even seen the doctor, who he hadn't seen for over five years.

Until this point, Tony had always been full of energy, fit, healthy and very rarely ill. He took pride in his health and fitness, and worked hard to maintain it. It was sad to witness such a healthy person suddenly experience daily pressure in his sinuses, eye, and headaches. He very rarely moaned, but you could see it was taking a toll on him.

One day, he opened up to me, and confessed he felt really annoyed with himself for having that vaccination, as he had felt ill ever since. "You did the right thing, for we took it to protect ourselves and others." I told him. "I know, Jane but the pressure in my head is constant and I felt so well before," he said.

I knew he had been struggling, yet it made me sad to hear it was constant. Tony is a man of few words and very rarely complains, just gets on with things. I asked him if he would like some healing, as I knew he would never ask. He accepted, to my surprise. We sent the kids away to their rooms, and told them under no circumstances they were to come downstairs until I had finished the healing.

As soon as I mentioned the word healing, a couple of them rolled their eyes and looked amused that their dad had brought into mum's craziness. I explained the process then told Tony to relax and try and enjoy the experience. The healing began. It was stronger than usual, and I noticed the beautiful, elegant black lady was working with me. My hands moved around his energy, as I was led directly to his head.

I was shown previous hairline fractures around his face, beneath his eye sockets. I knew these were from his younger days playing sports. His sinuses were so inflamed and angry, it was no surprise he was getting headaches. At the top of his nose, between his eyes, the tissues looked messy and full of zigzag scar tissue. I was shown his jaw was very slightly out.

Another healer, who I immediately recognised, stepped into the energy. This healer does surgical work. I know. Crazy right? But it's the truth.

He passed to me a long, sharp metal needle device which we used to gently place within Tony's sinuses area, and then suctioned out the damaged tissues, making healthy space for the sinuses to function properly.

After this, a grey clay substance was pushed gently into the old hairline fracture cracks to strengthen and support the eyes sockets and face. The forehead was cleansed with the sucking metal device, before supporting it with the grey clay for strength and protection. Next, gold energy was pushed into the entire area.

Finally, a blue substance was pushed through the head to reduce inflammation and discomfort. I heard clearly and firmly the word, "Enough!" When you hear this word, you are ordered to stop. I gently came out of the light trance, scanned over Tony's body to double-check if everything was okay.

I continued disconnecting and fully cleansing my energy, and following set procedures. I was shocked by the intensity of the healing session, and how much work was done and needed on Tony. I asked Tony afterwards whether he felt anything. A man of few words, he said, "Not really."

"Okay, so you felt nothing then? No heat, nothing?" I asked. "Well, I felt energy moving up and down my body, and a lot of heat in my head.

Oh yes, I felt my head was swirling and moving, but I knew I wasn't moving," he confirmed. "That's good. So you felt something then," I said. I noticed Tony was a little quieter than usual, as I could see he was trying to find logical explanations for the swirling movement inside.

I then explained he might feel a little off, emotional, and that it was completely different for everyone. I explained that the healing would continue until it was completed. He needed to relax, drink lots of water, and we would see how he felt. I explained I had seen lots of small hairline fractures around his face and eye socket.

Tony confirmed he had broken his nose and damaged all around his cheekbones when he was in his early twenties whilst playing football and it had been rather nasty. Well, I never knew that! We had a relaxing day, mostly sitting around the pool drinking water. So far, so good! It's the early hours of the morning, Tony is tossing and turning. He can't sleep.

He sat bolt upright and said, "Jane, I'm going downstairs. I've got a stabbing pain, throbbing pain in my head. I've never felt pain like it. I feel like I'm going to either pass out or be sick." I immediately jumped out of bed and got him some painkillers. He gingerly walks slowly down the stairs and looks white as a sheet.

"Shit, what have I done to him? Did I do too

much? Please let him be alright." I thought. Tony is sitting up on the couch, now looking grey, smiling gently, trying to reassure me he will be fine and for me to go back to bed. I'm lying in bed now praying to the divine, "Please let my Tony be okay. I'll work for you for eternity, in any capacity. But please, please, let my Tony get better."

Have I really hurt him? How can I continue healing if I can cause so much pain to another? I can't, I mustn't. I followed my guides, I stopped when told, what went wrong? It must have been me; my guides don't make mistakes. How could I have done this? I spend the whole night worrying whether Tony will be alive in the morning. What if he has a stroke?

I know what work we did inside his head, and it was extreme. Again and again, I resort to bargaining with the spirit world about how committed I am to work for the higher good of all, but please, please, please make my Tony okay. If you make my Tony okay, I fully promise not to question again and doubt my path. I must have passed out and fallen asleep.

I wake up remembering the horror of what has happened. I lie there too scared to go downstairs and check on Tony. Will he still be alive? Thank goodness, he's alive! He still looks a little pale, but has a calmness around him. He says he feels better, just tired. Tony goes upstairs to lie down whilst I want to cry, for I've been so worried and genuinely thought I could have killed my husband. No exaggeration!

I can't heal anyone again if that is going to happen. I knew my healing had got stronger, but that's not right. I hear my thoughts, "Thank you. Thank you. Thank you!" I've made the promise, I'm fully onboard, thank you. I feel emotionally exhausted, I am about to burst into tears of gratitude before I hear, "Mum, have you seen my swimsuit?" Back in the material world.

Over the next few days, I notice Tony is picking up with energy and looking healthier. I ask him how he feels. "Okay, Jane, I'm not exaggerating. I have never experienced pain like it, my head felt like it was going to explode. I was frightened," he said. I don't remember, in over twenty plus years, Tony ever used that word, and certainly not to describe himself.

I remind him he needs to take it easy for the next few days before I say, "So Tony, when would you like another healing?" "Never!" He replies. On a positive, I always like to finish on a positive, I realised just how much I really do love him. I'm contacted by someone to do some healing, but declined.

I can't heal anymore if it could hurt someone. I need to understand why this occurred, so I decided to write. I'm told not to doubt spirit. I will only be able to channel exactly what is right for the person. Well, that doesn't bring me much comfort, for as much as I believe in them, there could possibly be a weakness in the team, me!

After a few weeks, I do a healing on a family member being completely honest and open with my concerns. "I believe in you and know you would never hurt me," said a family member. Somebody not only believes in me, but loves me enough to allow me anywhere near them after what I have just admitted. How amazing is that?

I send up thoughts before I begin the healing that it must be taken down a gear and this person will only receive gentle healing. Now I know this isn't how it works, as my team is completely in control, and I'm just the channel. But it makes me feel better. The healing is administered, and I'm pleased to say that the person's physical discomfort improved and had no awful affects.

After a couple more healings, I started to question myself less. Still, the memory of Tony's healing had left a little self-doubt. After a full month of doing the healing on Tony, he finally admitted he hadn't had any more episodes of debilitating pain in his head. He admitted he hadn't had a headache since I had done healing on him.

"Why didn't you say anything earlier? I've been

questioning whether I should continue to heal. You had such a bad reaction, I thought I had done something wrong," I told him. "Well, I was waiting to see if the headaches would come back. I was checking it wasn't just a coincidence. It's been over a month, and my symptoms haven't come back so I thought I should mention it," he said.

"Tony, do you think the healing had anything to do with it?" I asked. "Well, I haven't had that awful pressure or headaches since, so there must be something in it?" Tony said. "Tony, it would have been nice to have known a little sooner," I said. "I know, but I didn't want to say anything until I was sure it wasn't going to come back and it wasn't just a placebo effect."

Really! I understand Tony isn't comfortable or hundred percent convinced with how I work, as it makes no logical sense to him, which I respect. I have a feeling though, he is very slowly being converted!

FEARS SURFACING

I go through occasional sporadic horrendous dreams. There is no warming or logical sense of why and when I receive them. These dreams are so vivid, upsetting and can be terrifying. I like to think of these dreams as removing layers of perhaps, previous lives' fears, that haven't been fully processed or buried so deep it's time they come up for air to be heard. This is my dream. Tony thinks I'm cheating on him.

In the dream, I look guilty, and I'm surrounded by evidence that screams loud and clear I've been unfaithful. He is standing in the distance with the rest of my family, as this accusation has driven a wedge between the family. I'm contemplating whether I should actually cheat on Tony as I've already been found guilty, so I've nothing to lose. I stood directly in front of Tony, as I can physically hear his choked, tearful voice, desperately fighting back the tears. "Jane, why would you treat me like this?" He asked.

"I haven't." I reply, but then question could I in the future? Again and again, dreams of insecurity of betrayal within our marriage. The dream continues where my mum is dying, then one of my children. I'm sobbing and retching so hard, I can physically feel pain in my chest. There's this pain buried so deep within my soul, and it simply won't release. I need to get out of this dream.

I've become, over the years, able to work with lucid dreams, steering them in a more positive direction, or at least taking a little control. I'm fighting to rectify the damage, cruelty and heartache of this dream, but I can't. I'm losing everything. My family is falling and spiralling before my eyes, and there is nothing I can do. The physical pain is exhausting. Again and again, I'm feeling this deep retching buried within.

I can hear a harrowing scream of deep despair, pain, and suffering. I have never heard such a harrowing cry of deep sadness. Where is this sound coming from? It's coming from me! The pain and nausea continues to pull at my soul. I need to be sick. My heart has broken. I'm searching within the dream frantically to escape. It hurts so much the grief of losing loved ones.

I'm screaming deep within. No sound, just the heartache and pain filling every cell and fibre within my body. I've broken free! I've escaped the dream. I'm lying there still, heart racing and horrified. I feel great sadness and my chest feels physically fatigued from all the hurt, grief and turmoil.

I contemplate what has just occurred. Firstly,

I'm grateful that I was fortunate enough to experience this sorrow through a dream, and not in this reality. Secondly, as I'm fully aware each one of us will mourn the passing of another, and no one is exempt. I need to understand why I need to sense, feel, see and hear so vividly within my dreams. I'm simply told, layers are being removed.

You cannot bury and hide previous or existing emotions from yourself. Hide them from others if you choose, but you can't hide them from yourself. Fears, if not processed, will always surface to the top. These dreams are upsetting, yet each time I have one, I simply look at it, as old layers that are being removed so new layers can grow. I used to panic and wonder if I was having a premonition, but found this too exhausting and negative.

Nobody can predict the future one hundred percent. It's up to a higher divine source. Our job whilst we are lucky to be here, is to love everyone as best we can. Take nothing for granted, and enjoy whatever time we have. No day should pass with unresolved words. I will only wish well for others and always find forgiveness within my heart.

I will not have any regrets, not in this lifetime. Clearing out as I call it, can be challenging, however over time, I have learnt it is needed. I have noticed when I make a significant higher shift spiritually, it is often, although not always, followed by a period of unpleasant clearing dreams. The body, mind and spirit need to heal before it can progress forward. Just an observation.

THE TIDE IS TURNING

Whilst spending time in my daily practice of meditative/trance state, I have noticed the veil between me and the spirit world feels even closer. The energy feels denser, closer, more material, verging as one. I have no proof, other than a strong knowing my spirit team is working relentlessly to perfect our connection. Yes, I'm the channel, but they are the ones perfecting and working out how best to use me safely.

It's as though a whole team of highly advanced intellectual, engineering, and scientific beings are finely monitoring and perfecting our connection. Since the experience from the holiday, my energy feels different. I feel more advanced, powerful and strong. It also feels foreign. I need time for my body, mind, and spirit to adapt. I know I can't push through this chapter, as I'm fully aware I must go with it until it becomes my normal.

My brain feels fatigued as I'm experiencing sensory overload due to everyday light and sounds. I've been having flashing images of past trauma which I thought I had processed. Mentally, hand on heart, I can say, I feel at peace with my entire past. I feel thankful for everything, for I appreciate this is part of my story.

I'm also fully aware I have this slight heaviness upon my chest which I've tried everything to release, but it is firmly embedded. Why? I don't know. Whilst in my meditative state, I ask my guides to free me from this memory and to reconnect me to the innocent child who was carefree. Let the adult and the child, finally free from any heartache, guilt and despair from this lifetime and previous.

I ask to be shown what it is that keeps me tied to this. I expect nothing and know I will only receive it when the time is right. I'm drifting deeper into a meditative state and can feel the familiar presence of my guides. I'm so safe and protected, as I happily go deeper into the beauty of nothingness. Images of memories are shown clearly, before I'm made fully aware it is me, that is stopping my freedom to escape the perils of guilt, dirt and darkness.

The pain in the left side of my head and chest is riddled with pain due to me imprisoning myself. How can this be? I feel fine with my past. I'm made aware, although my intellectual mind has moved forwards, the physical fibres have held on tight. I'm fascinated and intrigued by how powerful the body is to hold onto memories.

Maybe that is why so many never fully heal, after

spending hours on therapy. Mentally processing and accepting, yet not physically allowing the whole person to heal. This made perfect sense, for others I have helped heal, but I'd never given myself the same time or consideration to fully heal. This all made sense. "Discipline," I heard clearly.

I was losing the connection to the spirit world by allowing my thoughts to enter. I submerge myself immediately back into the still, silence, and calmness of nothingness. My jaw starts to be manipulated into strange positions as I hear the sound of grinding bones. My shoulders and head are elevated, as my head is shaken from side to side, violently releasing the jaw and facial muscles. The manipulations grind to a halt.

I sense two tall, strong, dark Equilibrium beings standing on either side of my upper body. They draw closer into my energy, resulting in the usual eerie calmness. I lay perfectly still as a large, bony, grey, slightly transparent hand hovers over my third eye. My jaw has a mind of its own as it's being moved in aggressive sharp, quick movements before my head is shaken rapidly from side to side.

This time, I can feel fluid moving within and around my head, down both sides of my neck. Shivers of cold energy running repeatedly down my spine to the bottom of my feet. Next, I feel waves of warmth and pleasure as tears stream down my face. I'm overwhelmed. I'm overcome with pure love, contentment and total acceptance. I hear the words, "You are strong and a warrior."

I then repeated, "I am strong, I am a warrior." Time stood still. I feel courageous, strong and a true warrior that has already conquered. I cannot falter off this path, for I have already succeeded. I can see a thin, grey, transparent web veil being removed from my physical and spiritual bodies.

I hear the words, "The time is now, the end is near." These words came from the Equilibriums, which startled me a little. I fully came out of the meditative state before sending gratitude and love. As I lay there, I said to myself quietly, "I hope so."

ADAPTING TAKES TIME

The dreams have settled down. I feel different. My energy, strange choice of words, doesn't feel as though it's fully mine. I'm out walking with my dog, Lottie, surrounded by the beautiful, calming, and uplifting woods. I always feel at my happiest when I walk in nature. I find myself breathing deep breaths and stopping to stare at the natural beauty of what this land should naturally look like.

I love the sounds of the birds, rustling of the leaves and the fresh wind upon my face. Today, I feel weird and cumbersome. My body feels stretched, I feel so tall, as though I'm seven feet tall. I'm struggling to walk properly and naturally. Less time looking at nature and more concentration on where I'm putting my feet. As I look down at my feet, they look too small to be manoeuvring this long, thin, ridiculously tall body.

I've experienced this sensation before, but not to the point where I'm concerned I'm going to bump into another person and look like I've been taking something. I identify there is an Equilibrium being in my energy. First, I ask if I am correct, my throat immediately constricts, letting me know that I am right. I firmly ask the Equilibrium to move further away from my energy as it's too extreme.

The sensation reduces to the point, I feel fully back in my own body and walking normally. I can still feel the strong presence, and can see out of the corner of my eye, glimpses of a tall dark shadow. I'm comfortable with that, starting to get used to it. I wonder why the Equilibrium is encroaching into my space.

"Protection!" I hear clearly. My inquisitive mind already knows that, but why do I need heightened protection? I decided to simply accept, as I know, when the time is right, it will all come to light!

A PLEASANT SURPRISE

It has been just over three months since I was last contacted and received healing from the healer. This lady contacts me when she is given permission from the spirit world. I'm only to receive healing at exactly the right time. Isn't that morally brilliant? A healer that trusts her guides and is led by a pure healing source. Maybe frustrating for the person receiving healing, as we are all guilty of wanting to heal as quickly as possible.

You can't rush healing for we are all different and receiving multiple healing sessions doesn't guarantee quicker results. I know from experience working with spirit, they let you know when and how much time is required between healing sessions. I love the way this woman works, authentic and true to her high moral values and dedicated to helping others. This lady is in demand and could easily become consumed with wealth, but chooses not to.

I've never met a talented healer that has stayed completely committed to her purpose. Some would say a gift from God. I would agree. A distance healing time and date is agreed. The healing is about to begin so I go upstairs, lie on the bed, and relax. I must explain, I know a lot of healers, but I wouldn't allow any of them near me, unless firstly, I had been given permission from my guides, and secondly their energy felt pure.

Finding a selfless pure healer is literally gold dust. I can feel my guides surrounding me, letting me know I am fully protected. As I allow myself to go into a deeper meditative state, I send up a thought asking my guides to work with this lady to progress my healing forwards. As I'm lying there, I can feel the healer channelling healing into my upper back.

A strong comforting warmth radiates across my upper back and chest, before travelling down my spine. The pleasant heat is penetrating deep within the left side of my rib cage, as I feel this gentle, loving warmth, touching my heart and the structures around it. The left side of my head feels like it is swirling, as I'm shown images of the top centre of my skull trying to be energetically realigned.

I'm so relaxed I can feel myself going deeper and deeper into a trance state. I can feel the right side of my head being worked on. I'm overcome with a blissful sensation of peace. I'm bathing in the warmth and light touch of an intense healing power. I'm drifting off and have no desire to take control.

I wake up from such a deep state, and have no idea how long I have been out of it. I'm wondering whether the healer has finished. As I'm about to sit up and check the time, I'm firmly told to stay still. The energy suddenly becomes stronger, more powerful, and different. My guides step in closer, reassuring me I am safe, protected and it is vital that I stay still.

As I lie there, I can feel a covering of what feels like a light blanket of web woven of thin hair, covering my entire body. It's so intricate and delicate, this banket of thin weblike hair, that it appears and feels like a transparent veil of matter. The intensity and weight of this blanket is somehow holding me down. I'm fully aware this is not the time to move.

I'm completely calm and compliant as I physically feel something touching and pushing my forehead down towards the bed, naturally elongating my neck. This causes a swirling sensation within the left side of my body, causing increased unpleasant pressure, creating a swooshing noise in my left ear.

I can feel the left and right side of my body trying to find a healthy balance. I'm swirling as both sides are trying to work out stability and the correct healthy balance for the body to comply and heal. Suddenly my head lifts up, chin tilts to the left, as my head flicks up forcing my mouth open and the jaw feels like it has been repositioned.

The swooshing noise in my left ear disappears. I'm still unable to move. The movements in my head, neck and jaw start again, however this time very gently. The movements are precise, so gentle and controlled, fascinating to experience. Eventually the healing stops. I gingerly get out of bed to check the time.

The healing started at 10.30 a.m. and usually, is finished at the latest within an hour. The time is 12.25 p.m., I've lost time. I ring the healer, and apologise for not contacting her sooner, before explaining what occurred. She is completely unfazed and reiterates just how intense and strong the energy was whilst healing me.

I then shared the images of previous past lives in great detail, including the raw sense of pain and heartache still held within my chest area. The healer revealed what she had seen, felt, and knew. She confirmed the past lives I had seen were from the Atlantean times. I had heard others talk about Atlantis, but knew nothing about it other than apparently, people who used to live there were advanced healers, and the island was destroyed and apparently underwater.

That was my total knowledge. I had no interest in it, for it didn't affect me. The healer continues.

Apparently, my original ancestral family came from Atlantis. My family were highly thought of and well-respected. They were known as the most gifted light healers at that time. They were so spiritually aware and advanced in their knowledge that they could create supernatural phenomena.

They strived to work with the loving divine source to spread light. When Atlantis was destroyed, they, out of all the people, should have happily walked into the light and trusted in the Divine. Just before the final collapse, they doubted! They let a doubting mind and heart fuel their fear. This was a huge sin for such enlightened, wise and loving people for they, more than anyone, knew the truth.

The truth that love and light lay ahead of them, they doubted! This doubt has led to a deep embedded doubt in the future lives, for the ancestral family line. This apparently is connected to me. The healer explained she saw a chest buried deep within the bottom of the ocean, with four lights surrounding it. She continued to explain there should be twelve. The chest has been discovered, but it is not ready to be opened. This will take more time.

In time, this would be unravelled, but it was up to me to pray and work with a person called Padre Pio to confess the sins and doubting minds and hearts of my ancestral family. What the heck! Can nothing be straightforward? I ask the healer who Padre Pio is. I have never heard of him. Basically, in simple terms, he is a holy Italian priest with stigmata, and healed others.

He is well known for doing miracles. He had mystical gifts such as reading souls, healing, removing darkness, and could see the spiritual side. He was able to see Jesus and Mary as a child. He brought back many to their faith. Did I mention he was a Catholic priest? I mention to the healer, "Oh, my mum will be delighted that I need to reconnect to the catholic faith for I've spent so long avoiding it."

I need to digest all this information for it all seems too difficult to believe. Is there any substance and truth to what I've been told? My logical mind screams this is silly. But my gut, inner knowing automatically knows this lady only speaks the truth, and as much as I want to deny what I've heard, I know it is the truth! I'm advised to spend time connecting with Padre Pio, perhaps through a letter or just going into the quiet to connect and find forgiveness.

I cannot move forward until the past is forgiven. Once again, I repeat, I need time to step back and review what has just happened. I will admit that throughout this lifetime, I had always suffered with self-doubt.

It didn't matter how much I would often overachieve, there was always this perpetual self-doubting heart. As silly as this might sound, what the healer has unravelled resonates with me on a deeper level. I'm starting to understand myself.

FORGIVENESS TAKES TIME

After the healing session, I struggled to sleep. Once finally asleep, I wake up on the dot at 4 a.m. due to awful lucid dreams. The same topic each time, I can't protect my loved ones. There are always children within the dream, where I'm fighting off the darkness, desperately protecting the innocence and purity of the children. Lucid dreams feel as real as the material world.

I'm taken to dark, seedy places where there is no care or consideration for life. Children are treated like animals, no consideration for their emotional well-being. I'm in a dirty, crammed, metal barred crate, with several other women hugging their children, reassuring them they will be okay. As I look down, I see I'm hugging two of my children, as they are cowering and clinging onto my body.

I can physically feel their small bodies clinging onto me. My children are aged four and six, so fully aware of what is taking place. Their faces are pale with fear as they remain shocked with fright. "It's okay, mummy is here, I'll protect you." I comfort them knowing fully aware, I am powerless. I feel sick to my stomach, my heart is racing whilst I put on a brave face, smiling gently at my two children's innocent faces.

I'm trapped in a situation where there is nothing I can do. Other children are being snatched, screaming as they are forced out of their helpless crying mother's arms. The aggressive men are working their way down the line, eyeing up the children for financial gain. I can feel the constant perpetual fear, anxiety, and heart-wrenching pain of all the children and mothers.

The crying penetrated through my physical body. I need to protect the innocent, but how? The men imprisoning us, have weapons and are stronger than us. I must do something, for death would be a more humane and kinder outcome. I'm racking my brain, but the torture and self-doubt of feeling so weak, useless and powerless is stronger. I know the future of these gentle souls. I must do something to save them.

This cannot be! I'm fighting desperately to get out of this dream. I'm forbidden, made to watch, and to feel remorse. A punishment unbearable, I'm made to watch and feel the heightened fear, terror, and cruelty of others. I woke up! Exactly 4 a.m. My heart and chest is hurting, as though I've been physically retching. I find myself lying still with my hands directly over my heart, praying to Padre Pio for forgiveness.

I plead for forgiveness for my ancestral family and my doubting heart. I ask for strength, courage, and to conquer these vile, vivid dreams. I understand and accept the doubting mind and heart of my ancestral family that would have created lifetimes of pain and suffering for others and that we are truly sorry. I return to a calmer light state, but never return fully back to sleep.

These dreams continue for several days. At exactly 4 a.m. I wake up, often covered in sweat due to witnessing the dark, evil treatment of innocent people. I'm feeling sleep deprived, yet I know this process is part of stripping back previous layers from this life and many before. All shadows of self-doubt and hidden fears are being removed.

I'm reflective and thankful for the experience for if my ancestral family due to their doubting hearts have caused others pain, then it must be rectified. Past wrong behaviour must be acknowledged and learnt from. Hopefully in time, forgiven, for all to move forwards. How did I get in the middle of all of this? Perhaps a coincidence?

I don't believe coincidences are true. Each morning at 4 a.m., I continue to pray for forgiveness. After a week, the lucid dreams vanish. I sleep content throughout the night, feeling refreshed in the morning. I wonder, have we been forgiven? Only time will tell. For now, I'm thankful to escape those dreams.

I pray for any others seeking forgiveness, or those trapped in time, a dream or reality. Positive healing thoughts are sent out into the universe. I hope I have done enough, for I have never felt so remorseful for my ancestral family's behaviour and our doubting hearts.

A NEW MEMBER

I continue my everyday life, however I have noticed random images of a male presence, as though trying to get my attention. I have seen this gentleman before, years ago, but thought nothing of it. He presents himself as an Indian, wearing very little other than a white turban, and some sort of loincloth. I think he is Hindu, as I can see a clear red spot directly on his forehead.

He is an older gentleman, with a grey beard. He looks weathered with deep lines on his face. Sometimes he has white powder covering him, other times, he hasn't. His energy, when near, feels very strong, clear, pure, precise and magical. What do I mean by magical? I have this knowing he can do things that are even more advanced in healing.

I don't know what they are, but he is persistently getting into my energy. I'm intrigued, I don't push it for I know to let things unravel naturally. Whilst meditating, he appears clearly to me. I find myself staring deep into his gentle, serious, deep brown eyes. I'm made fully aware he knows everything about me, my strengths, weaknesses and capabilities. He feels incredibly familiar. Where do I know him from?

A previous life perhaps, for I haven't known him in this lifetime. I feel comforted by his presence, all knowing, calm, and protection. I have this impulse to put my hands over my lower pelvis. The intensity and heat coming from my hands is multiplied, filling my entire body with a strong, loving, heat.

I can feel muscular fibres and structures moving within my body, as if making a clear entrance for energy to flow. I'm fully aware he is using me as a channel to self-heal. His healing is powerful and physically in this world, stronger than anything I have felt. As he continues to work with me, the veil between us feels so thin he could be standing in the room. I can sense the presence of my other guides surrounding him, yet they are standing further back observing.

The healing continues as my hands are guided to specific areas of my body so he can filter through his energy. The healing comes to an end. "Bloody hell, that was strong! I hope I can use his healing when helping others," I think instantly. Whilst doing healing for a fellow medium, I can see clearly this healing guide step directly into my energy. Once again, I can see the other healing guides, but he seems to be taking the lead - "Magic man."

I decided that's what I'm going to call him. As I drift into a deeper trance, he leads me to certain parts of the medium's body. The other guides come in at specific points using their expertise. A perfect team working in harmony, respectful of one another's healing roles. The medium needed deeper, more magical healing to aid her to move forwards in her spiritual growth.

At the end of the session, just before I disconnect fully, I find myself overcome with happiness as I look at the seven healing guides surrounding me. The realisation that my team is fully complete. There will be other sacred and divine beings in the future to aid the journey, yet these are the main seven and won't change.

I'm overcome with a sensation of completeness. I feel the finish line of this chapter is within touching distance. The beauty of channelling healing for a fellow medium is, you can be totally open and honest when describing their healing session at the end. The medium immediately identified the healing, felt so much stronger, verging on not as comfortable as previous healings.

She explained it was very intense and powerful as her whole body felt as though it was expanding. She found it interesting that deep within her right ear was being worked on. She went on to explain this was the area where she suffered from migraines. I knew she had suffered from migraines, but she had never mentioned her symptoms. Mediums can be cagey, and don't tell you everything about themselves.

This is a habit most of us have, being a little more reserved. I know it is because we are all searching for evidence. We are intrigued in each other's healing abilities and like others, mediums need proof as well. This fascinated her, she seemed reflective and a little quieter than normal. She already knew the power and capability of spirit, but had now physically felt the precise technique I was working with.

I confirmed to her I had been working with a new healer and had found the healing overall felt more powerful. She agreed and then said, "I don't know where this is going Jane, but it's certainly going somewhere, that is a fact."

CONTACTED OUT OF THE BLUE

A family has been having strange occurrences taking place in their new home. Objects like cardboard boxes moving across the entire length of a room without any logical explanation. The children feel unsettled, yet can't articulate why. The kind family fosters a dog, they are experienced dog owners with a wealth of knowledge, but unfortunately, the dog can't settle, becoming agitated.

It's blatantly clear the dog can't cope with the energy in the house, so they have to return it. Lots of different, strange incidents occur which they all come up with explanations, although not very convincing. The mother of the house is having a relaxing bath, when all of a sudden, the bathroom cabinet door flies open, and a candle slides off the shelf, smashes into the sink, and breaks the entire sink base.

She jumps out of the bath, desperately scientifically trying to work out how the candle managed to open a sturdy cabinet door, slide off a stable shelf and break the sink. It has become too much, she seeks logical explanations, but this time she knows there is something eerie, creepy, and energetically not right in this house!

This is the lady that contacts me. I listen intensely to her situation, and have no desire to get involved. I know straight away the energy of the house is not right. I can see an image of a female spirit child, which needs returning to the correct time and place. The child doesn't feel threatening, but the energy in the house feels off. Seems straightforward.

I'm still reluctant to get involved, but then my throat constricts, as I'm made fully aware, I am to help. The lady goes on to tell me how it is affecting her children. Why did she mention that? I was happily detached up until that part. I tell her I'll have a think about what is going on and whether there is anything I can do to help her. I'll contact her as soon as I know more.

What I'm actually doing is double checking with my guides whether it is safe and morally correct for me to get involved. I won't lie, I have no interest in doing any form of house clearing as it usually consists of unpleasant energy, and I don't want to put myself in harm for others, unless I'm specifically guided to. There are people out there that specialise in this sort of stuff, not me. No thank you!

I ask my guides what I should do and I'm told immediately, I have to help. This has been engineered for your progression. Really! You know I have no interest in working in this way. "You must, Jane," my guides told me. "Will I be protected?" I asked. "Yes, one hundred percent. We will not allow any harm to come to you," my guides replied. Then I find myself sounding like a broken record, constantly asking and checking whether they are sure with this decision.

There is no doubt, I am here to help this lady. I tune in to see if I can find out what is causing the disruption in this house, and can see in my mind's eye, a small girl hidden in a dark space, frightened. I ask my guides if that is her true identity and if she is a pure soul. I'm told I am correct. I think to myself, "This looks straightforward enough."

I presume a simple soul rescue should sort it out, and I'm feeling rather confident. However, I have this nagging, unsettled feeling, but why? So, I contacted the lady and agreed to help her. We arrange a time and date where there will be no one in the house, so I can remotely enter her home.

She sends me a video link of her entering her front door and going into each room. I don't usually ask for this but have been guided to. Why? I'll find out. I have this strange, ominous feeling inside, it is vital I check every corner of the house.

THE DAY OF RECKONING

I won't lie, I'm not feeling over excited with the prospect of remotely going inside another person's house to remove, I strongly suspect, an element of dark energy. Who knows I might get a surprise and be completely wrong. I check in with my guides several times to check whether I should really be working in this way. I'm told firmly that I must!

Now I know morally it's the right and kind thing to do, but surely, they could have found another person to do this. Some brave, overexcited warrior who wants to banish all evil. Someone, anyone rather than me. Right, moan over. I have a final strong word with myself, "Right Jane, pull yourself together. You are fully protected. Get on with it."

I open the video link sent by the owner of the house, and my entire body fills with dread and a physical repulsion towards the home. Every room needs clearing, but upstairs, the energy feels darker, more dangerous, and pure evil. "Bloody great!" I think to myself. I remind myself this has come to me for a reason, and I'm totally protected.

I also know once I'm in the trance state, I work within, my guides will immediately step in. They are powerful, true warriors, and nothing has direct access to me. Here goes. I go into a light meditative state, breathing slowly, feeling myself going further and further into trance. I feel the presence of my guides as I smile with contentment.

I send up my intention to remove all energy from previous lives to the present moment that does not belong or serve in love and light, the people within this house, now! As soon as I've said the words, I'm remotely viewing inside the woman's house. When I do remote viewing, it is as though I am physically there. Straight away, I feel Medicine man enter my energy.

He surrounds me with his protective and very strong presence. I know from experience he only steps in when dark energy needs to be eliminated. I blend with his energy going a little deeper into trance, as I hear myself making strange, loud, and then softer breathing noises like a slow, strong siren. I'm feeling mighty, brave, and aggressively powerful, as I sense the darkness, corruption, and seediness as though seeping within the walls.

All fear has vanished as I become focused, determined and hungry in search of the enemy. My arms automatically start to rotate in circular movements in front of my body, as though creating energy into a fast swirling and spiralling funnel. I can see a funnel of swirling indigo blue expanding as my arms go faster and faster. The funnel of dark indigo air is complete, it looks like you would imagine a small hurricane.

We walk through the hallway into the kitchen on the left and push with our hands the fast-rotating funnel of air into the centre of the room. The funnel removes what looks like hundreds of pieces of debris and a dark sludge substance from within the atmosphere as though fully deep cleansing the room. It seems to take a long time as the black sludge substance is reluctant to move.

Before we enter the next room, there is a mirror directly in front of us. Medicine man immediately throws a black cloak/cloth over it to prevent any energy from being able to expand or magnify in strength against us. We walk calmly and methodically into each room creating further funnels of swirling air/energy specifically to remove stagnant and dark energy that is not welcome.

The energy feels stagnant like patches of mould left too long seeping up the walls, draining the house of energy and vitality. This darkness has been feeding off the previous owner's energy, fuelling, and entwining within their lives, increasing negativity and misery. So far so good, it all feels straightforward. The energy has rapidly shifted. There is a sense of danger and emergency as Medicine man's energy is heightened.

My head and eyes are rotating faster from side to side as though frantically searching for predators. Something is hiding and watching us. We start to walk upstairs; I see within my mind's eye a dark red substance as though leaking tears of blood from the walls. The house feels riddled with dark evilness as though walking through stifling, thick, smoggy air. The energetic atmosphere of the home feels vile.

"Discipline!" I hear clearly. This is not a time to lose focus as this will empower the other side. We walk into the first room, it feels okay. A funnel is created to cleanse the entire room. Just as we are about to leave, I catch a glimpse of a rusty, brown, orange reflection under the bed. As I crouch down to look, something is staring directly at me. It scuttles further under the bed trying to hide itself.

It doesn't feel pleasant, but also not dangerous and threatening. I crouch down onto my knees gently signalling with my arms it is safe to come out. Medicine man steps in and puts a transparent barrier between me and this thing.

I still can't fully see it, as it's cowering in a hunched-up ball position. I remain calm, relaxed, and gentle telling it, it's safe to come out. It bravely looks directly at me, trying to figure out whether it's safe.

Finally, it gingerly pokes its head out before fully coming from under the bed. I have never seen anything like this. It is tiny, less than a metre in height, painfully thin, malnourished, with fragile paper-thin skin. It has a bald head with patches of sporadic hairs. It has large dark eyes, with a tiny lump resembling the nose with two holes and a small mouth with no pigmentation around it.

It has characteristics like a human, yet it's not. The creature feels sick, poorly, and looks riddled with disease and ill-health. There is no spark of hope or light within this creature, as though it has accepted its fate. I catch another glimpse of light reflecting from under the bed, several more pairs of eyes are staring directly at me. There are more! There are too many to count. I hold the energy as I can see Medicine man creating a separate funnel.

The tiny creatures are intrigued by my presence as they very slowly start to come towards me. Through my mind's eye, I'm somehow gently gathering them all up from around the back, side, and under the bed, creating an energetic pen as though herding up cattle. Once all safely in the pen, I show them the funnel Medicine man has created and tell them firmly, but gently they need to return to where they belong.

They do not belong here! They are frightened, untrusting and start to huddle up close together. Their energy isn't pure, more like a species who will do what they need to survive and at any cost. They could do good but also evil, whatever will benefit their needs. Basically, they are like vermin. They will attack and feed off whatever and whoever's energy to survive.

Suddenly I see clearly the presence of a tall, dark Equilibrium being, towering over the entire room. The Equilibrium being remains silent, simply points with its bony, pale long finger to the funnel. The tiny creatures scuttle like a pack of rats into the funnel before it vanishes. I stood there, sensing if there was anything else remaining. Nothing, just calmness and normality. The Equilibrium has disappeared, all is eerily calm.

Time to move onto the next room. This room feels okay. I'm made aware that the child who sleeps in this room has the ability and spiritual gifts to keep dark energy away. A funnel is created to cleanse the whole room thoroughly before moving on to the next room. The next room feels full of fear created by the sensitivity and awareness of the child who this bedroom belongs too.

The child feels and knows that this house to them doesn't feel right. My eyes are drawn to the ceiling, letting me know we need to cleanse the loft. My arms rotate faster and faster in front of me as Medicine man uses me as a channel to create another funnel of swirling air in a lighter shade of blue. All the present fear created is magnified before illuminating the whole room in a beautiful sky-blue colour as though being healed.

Sparks of golden light, with flickers of blue, rain down from the ceiling, cleansing and healing the area. Time to move on. Literally as I step through the next bedroom door, I'm hit with a thick, smoggy, stale and stagnant energy. It feels suffocating with a mixture of advanced spiritual wisdom and negativity. "What is this?" I ask. I'm shown a symbol of a star within an old-fashioned book of scriptures. I don't recognise it.

I'm made aware the child without knowing it, has either been drawing the symbol or subconsciously knows of it. This child has a natural spiritual ability to do what? I don't know nor does the child yet, but it's strong. The dark beings within this house have manipulated the wisdom of this child to gain further strength within the home. Medicine man steps in closer,

I'm told to detach all emotions and to focus. I ask, "Does this child need healing?"

I hear firmly and with authority, "DETACH NOW!" The sense of urgency intensifies. I need to remain in the energy, cleanse the room, and move on. A funnel is placed in the room to cleanse the space. As we step out of the bedroom, we seal off the entire room to protect the rest of the house and the family members. The child is very spiritually gifted, but we haven't been given access to how the child might choose to use the gifts in the future.

The bedroom is sealed off, simply as a precaution to prevent any more disruptions within the home. I feel the need to spend more time helping the child as my natural maternal instincts kick in. "Move on!" Medicine man told me firmly. Medicine man knows my weakness better than me but will not tolerate any form of vulnerability when we are working.

Focused, emotionally detached, and verging on robotic as we enter the final room. The room feels eerily calm yet normal. We stand there scanning the room, something doesn't feel right, but what? I can feel Medicine man focused and refusing to move. We stood still as our eyes continued to search the room. Nothing! Suddenly out of the corner of my eye, I can see what looks like a dark shadow crawling up the wall and expanding over the entire ceiling.

I turn my head to look as I see this dark shadow substance trying to encase us. I feel strange, a little lightheaded, as though this dark energy is trying to infiltrate and gain access to my energy. Medicine man informs me not to move, focus, and to hold the energy. Instantaneously like a bolt of lightning, Medicine man has pounced on the bottom of the black shadow substance and is aggressively pulling it down, yanking fiercely with brutal violence and force.

The large shadow upon the ceiling initially starts to recoil before growing in strength again. This dark energy feels enraged and powerful. Medicine man has created a large, dark, fast spiralling funnel which I can see peripherally. The energy of this dark shadow substance is powerful, all I can do is hold the energy, and refuse it access to grow. My feet are literally stuck to the ground as our energies are equal in strength. Stalemate!

I continue to hold the energy as Medicine man is yanking and dragging the dark substance towards the swirling funnel. Finally, the darkness upon the ceiling starts to reduce, as Medicine man continues to fight with this evil dark, treacle, energy sapping diseased substance. Within seconds the darkness completely vanishes into the funnel, as if into thin air.

The entire room returns to a surreal calmness and strange choice of words, peace. No time to reflect for the loft is calling. As we enter the dark loft, Medicine man is closely within my energy. I feel strong, powerful, fearless and excited to reveal what we will find. As we go in, I pick up the strong emotions of another. My stomach is full of fear, dread, and heightened anxiety.

I immediately identified this is not mine, but whose is it? I see a small girl, fair hair, not much older than five shaking in fear. She is sitting huddled in the corner of the loft hiding her face. Cautiously, we go a little closer as Medicine man reminds me, she might not be what she is presented as. Professional head on, as I remove all emotion. I have learnt from experience not everything we see in the spirit world is always its true identity.

Dark and evil energy can and will feed off kindness and vulnerability. I will not empower darkness. I slowly and very gently draw a little closer towards what appears to be a frightened child. I asked her softly to show me her eyes, but she refused. I crouch down and telepathically tell her she needs to be returned to where she belongs. She reluctantly, with fear, starts to raise her head.

I get a look directly into her eyes, she is an innocent child, petrified and trapped in time. I check with Medicine man if I am correct, he nods. My heart instantly softens as I know it is safe to drop the warrior energy to rescuer. As I smile softly at her, I say, "We are going to get you back home where you belong and can feel safe, happy, loved and looked after. Would you be okay with that?"

Literally, as I'm saying the words, several other children appear from all the corners of the loft, revealing their identity. The evil dark shadow energy had been feeding and growing in strength off these innocent children's fears. These pure, innocent children, trapped in a state of perpetual heightened horror of fear and anxiety. Children trapped in time, why, how this was able to occur, I don't know.

But I do know they will finally be freed. Medicine man has created a beautiful gold and silver funnel of fast swirling light. I'm asking one of my healing guides to step in to help me reassure the children. I'm refused and told it is time to do this myself. Medicine man has found and segregated some of those tiny, bald headed, painfully thin, ill looking creatures hidden amongst the children.

These creatures are like rats surviving off the children's terrors and fears. Medicine man creates a dark swirling funnel of what looks like a deep brown rustic air substance rotating rapidly. The vermin are removed into the funnel into the right time and dimension where they belong. The children and only these children are permitted to enter the pure brilliant gold, silver, bright light of this funnel.

As I gather up the children some of them are hesitant and untrusting. The braver children reassure them by holding onto one another's hands before stepping into the funnel. Eventually all the children are safely removed and returned to the light. A pure, loving light. I can't expand on this experience because that is all I'm permitted to know. I do know they are safe, loved, finally at peace and where they belong.

A haven where they can finally enjoy their journey. The house has returned to normal; the vibration has completely changed from one of horror to a new, blank canvas. A home is where you create your own energy, memories and stories. This house can now blossom into whatever the family wants. Before we depart, we place healing energy within and around the entire house and give thanks.

I return out of trance back into the here and now. I thoroughly wash my hands and forearms, disconnecting from any traces of other energies. I must now return to the spirit world for deep, proper cleansing to ensure my safety and health is fully protected. Unfortunately, lots of healers follow rituals they have learnt from others.

The reality is you can only be fully cleansed by the spirit world and will only learn this when it is shown and given to you. Some will disagree, that is your right. The most important thing is to be aware of different methods that work for you. Healing is a selfless gift to be used to help others, but it also comes with huge responsibility for self-care.

RETURNING TO THE SPIRIT WORLD

I send out my thoughts for cleansing, go into a light trance, and within seconds I'm back in the higher spiritual realms. I'm instantly met by the presents of my Indian guide which usually fills me with comfort and reassurance. The atmosphere feels strange, serious, as if almost formal. I'm put through the usual funnel of cleansing, swirling air encased in a transparent capsule.

I can feel and see through my mind's eye pieces of dark, dirty grime being removed out of my energy. The cleansing is complete as I step out of the transparent room/capsule. As I return to my guides, I can see they are all there, but have stepped further away from me making me fully aware this is not a time for interaction. I can see clearly a door that has been left open.

I turn to my Indian guide like an innocent child looking for reassurance. I stare into his gentle, loving brown eyes and say, "I Can't. I don't want to go through any more doors. I'm tired of feeling so poorly." He says nothing, simply looks at me with so much tender unconditional love. I turn and look at the door. The door is slightly open. I have a choice to stay as I am, or go through the next door.

I know I have got to go through the door for I have already seen the future. I step through the door. I can't see anything other than bright intense white. There is nothing, just me standing and surrounded by white. Nothingness! Pure white nothingness. As I look around, I eventually see the familiar tall, elegant, beautiful black lady which fills me with peace and comfort.

I feel my whole body encased in pure love. She just stands there and says nothing. I then see to my right another familiar being who presents as what you would imagine a mad science professor with unruly hair. I can't see anyone else, but I can feel the presence of many. The space feels packed with spiritual beings, more than I have ever experienced before. Why?

The black lady and the science professor start clapping. The whole atmosphere is filled with heightened joy and celebration. A strong sense of cheering, excitement and congratulations towards me! I can't see anything other than the black lady and the science professor. Nevertheless, the space feels jammed packed, busy with people/beings elated. As much as this is all very nice, I don't fully understand what is going on.

The professor purposely steps back, indicating

and making me fully aware there will be no more prodding and probing, for this section is complete. Everything is completed. I look to the strikingly beautiful black lady for explanation. "You are complete. You now have nothingness. A peace, calmness, and stillness deep within you. Nothingness."

"Your physical body is finally complete. Your journey will be one of hardship and there will be many challenges, but you now have nothingness! Stillness, calm, realignment of the physical, mental and spiritual bodies. Finally, your spirit is at peace, nothingness." As she said these words, I cried like an uncontrollable child. Suddenly a calm, nothingness filled the centre of my entire body with a peaceful, still, strong calmness of nothingness.

A sensation so pure, beautiful, and untainted. Pure love! The once, flow of uncontrollable tears instantly stopped. I then asked, "Can I still continue to work with my guides?" "If you want to," the black lady answered gently. "Yes, I do, I want to continue helping others, that is my desire. I want to do this for the rest of this life," I spoke passionately.

Intrigued by what had just occurred I had to ask the question. "So does this mean I will get completely better now?" The black lady looked me directly in the eyes and gently replied, "Yes, health and vitality. Isn't that what you have been asking for? Jane, you are to make a full recovery, but there are still a final few tweaks, this will take time." I pay my respects and thank everyone, including those who I'm not permitted to see.

I am fully aware there are many who have worked tirelessly, perfecting my healing, and the gifts I will go on to share with others. I am part of a team, the channel. One can't work without the other, and I'm humbled and grateful to be used in whatever method they have already decided for me. I know everything we do is pure, loving, and light.

I also know it is not for the faint-hearted, and is going to come with hardships and challenges that even I can't imagine. I am strong, I will not be defeated, and will fulfil this earthly journey. Some believe before we are born, we agree to our paths. Blimey, what was I thinking? I'll sit on the fence, until I'm shown differently. I leave the brilliant white room back through the door towards my guides. I'm greeted by them all, but it feels different.

I feel different, not so dependent on them, but more as an equal. I give my thanks and return to the material world. I'm back in the material world, sitting in my sitting room, but I don't want to come out of the safety and comfort of the energy. My chest feels so warm, as I can physically feel the sensation of a column or tube of warmth running from the top of my head down the entire length of my body.

The tube feels like a funnel of heated light, warming me up from the inside, radiating out. It feels strange, a little unusual, yet beautifully pleasant and comforting, as though I am being hugged. I sit and bathe in the warmth, longing for it to continue for as long as possible. Suddenly, an electrical shudder of energy shifts, as though my body has been realigned. I remain still, until I'm completely sure the process has been completed.

I fully come out of the meditative/light trance state and begin to gently move my body, connecting fully to the physical world. I can still feel the column or tube of energy working deep within the centre of my body. My body continues to feel embraced in an inner warm hug of healing energy. I feel different.

I feel emotional with joy and peace. I can't articulate the feeling other than, I feel complete! I'm happy with who I am and what I'm going to do in the future. For the first time in my life, I feel alive, excited by whatever earthly challenges are to come my way. At this precise time, fear no longer exists. I have just experienced pure love within. A deep inner silence, contentment, and blissful nothingness!

The End.

Printed in Dunstable, United Kingdom